# BUILDING A RESILIENT
# TWENTY-FIRST-CENTURY ECONOMY
# FOR RURAL AMERICA

# BUILDING A RESILIENT
## Twenty-First-Century Economy
# FOR RURAL AMERICA

### Don E. Albrecht

WESTERN RURAL DEVELOPMENT CENTER
UTAH STATE UNIVERSITY
*Logan*

Published by Utah State University Press
An imprint of University Press of Colorado
245 Century Circle, Suite 202
Louisville, Colorado 80027

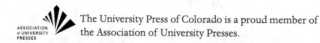 The University Press of Colorado is a proud member of
the Association of University Presses.

The University Press of Colorado is a cooperative publishing enterprise supported, in part, by Adams State University, Colorado State University, Fort Lewis College, Metropolitan State University of Denver, Regis University, University of Colorado, University of Northern Colorado, University of Wyoming, Utah State University, and Western Colorado University.

∞ This paper meets the requirements of the ANSI/NISO Z39.48–1992 (Permanence of Paper)

ISBN: 978-1-60732-986-2 (hardcover)
ISBN: 978-1-60732-941-1 (paperbook)
ISBN: 978-1-60732-951-0 (ebook)
https://doi.org/10.7330/9781607329510

Library of Congress Cataloging-in-Publication Data

Names: Albrecht, Don E., author.
Title: Building a resilient twenty-first-century economy for rural America / Don E. Albrecht.
Description: Logan : Utah State University Press, an imprint of University Press of Colorado, [2020] | Includes bibliographical references and index.
Identifiers: LCCN 2020014459 (print) | LCCN 2020014460 (ebook) | ISBN 9781607329862 (cloth) | ISBN 9781607329411 (paperback) | ISBN 9781607329510 (ebook)
Subjects: LCSH: Rural development—United States.
Classification: LCC HN59.2 .A42 2020 (print) | LCC HN59.2 (ebook) | DDC 307.1/412—dc23
LC record available at https://lccn.loc.gov/2020014459
LC ebook record available at https://lccn.loc.gov/2020014460

All cover images from Shutterstock.com. Left to right: © Oxford_shot; © Wingedbull; © Gitisak; © catalina.m

To the leaders and residents of rural America. I am impressed with your dedication and ingenuity as you work to address the serious and complex obstacles that confront your communities.

# Contents

# Acknowledgments

Many people have played a critical role in the development of this book and I couldn't have done it without them. First, I am very appreciative of the numerous residents, leaders, policy makers, and others who are working diligently to improve economic conditions in rural America. My confidence in humankind has been enhanced as I watch these people altruistically put in countless hours to help the residents of these areas. I have learned much from them, and this book is better because of their insights.

I really appreciate the staff at Western Rural Development Center (Betsy Newman, Deanna Thompson and Riana Gayle). They have done a great deal of work to make this book a reality. They have helped with data analysis, created graphs and charts, and kept the office running while I wander around the country. It is a privilege to work with such talented professionals.

I am fortunate to work with Rachael Levay and the staff at University Press of Colorado and Utah State University Press. They have been a great help to me every step of the way.

Finally, and most important, I wish to express my sincere appreciation to my wife, Carol Albrecht. As a sociologist, she has originated many of the thoughts expressed in this book. All of these ideas are more polished because I was able to discuss them with her as we drive together through rural America. Perhaps even more important, it is Carol and my family who make my life such a joy.

BUILDING A RESILIENT
TWENTY-FIRST-CENTURY ECONOMY
FOR RURAL AMERICA

# Introduction

The presidential election of 2016 brought the economic distress in rural America forcefully to the attention of the rest of the nation. Frustrated rural voters rejected the traditional platforms of both Republicans and Democrats and in overwhelming numbers cast their votes for political outsider Donald Trump. By winning a huge segment of the rural vote, especially in critical swing states such as Michigan, Pennsylvania, and Wisconsin, Trump was able to secure his surprise win.

The rural anger expressed in the 2016 election is largely a consequence of decades of economic stagnation and decline resulting from fewer jobs in the goods producing industries (manufacturing, construction and the natural resource industries of agriculture, logging, and mining). For example, since the 1970s, the number of jobs in manufacturing has declined by 7 million, 90 percent of coal-mining jobs have been lost, and there has been a 90 percent decline in the hours of farm labor required. Also, since 1990 two-thirds of the logging jobs have been lost. For the jobs that remain, wages in real dollars have declined (Autor and Dorn 2013; Autor et al. 2008). These trends are

DOI: 10.7330/9781607329510.c000

significant because these good-producing industries have traditionally been the most essential segment of the rural economy.

After decades of job loss and declining opportunities, many rural residents and other working-class voters were thrilled to hear the message of Donald Trump. Trump promised to bring back manufacturing, coal mining, and other jobs in the goods producing industries by taking a tough stand on immigration, by restructuring international trade agreements to protect American workers, and by eliminating restrictive environmental regulations.

The problem is that Trump's promises about restoring jobs in the goods producing sector simply cannot be fulfilled. His plans to build a wall, restrict immigration, restructure trade deals, and eliminate environmental restrictions will not bring these jobs back. The fact is that these policies do not address the base cause for the loss of jobs in the goods producing industries in the first place. Rather, the decline of jobs in the goods producing sector is primarily a consequence of technological changes. For decades, millions of jobs in agriculture, manufacturing, mining, and logging have been lost as ever-improving machines replace human labor in the production process (Albrecht 2014a; Rasker 2017). Critically, even though the number of workers in these industries is declining, production continues to increase.

Reductions in the number of jobs in the goods producing industries are a part of a massive industrial structure transformation brought about by advancements in technology. Not only are machines more efficient, but also advancements in information and communication technology have made these technological changes more dynamic. The result is that the United States and other nations around the world are transitioning from industrial economies to information- and service-based economies. Job skills in the goods producing industries that once provided a solid livelihood are becoming obsolete, and individuals who once held these jobs now find themselves unemployed or underemployed. No border wall or trade deal can prevent the continuation of this process. The same process is occurring in economically advanced nations throughout the world, and these nations are also dealing with the same feelings of anger and frustration among their residents.

Moreover, the impacts of technological change are spreading to other sectors of the economy. In the next few years, we can expect to lose millions of jobs in the retail sector as a result of online shopping and self-checkout technologies, and it is likely that millions of transportation jobs will be lost as self-driving vehicles replace truck and taxi drivers. In the emerging information and service economy, any job that consists of the same task being repeated over and over again is going to be replaced by a machine (Moretti 2012). While there are problems in using machines, employers often prefer a technical solution if it is available. While machines occasionally break down, they don't get sick, tired, distracted, fail to show up for work, ask for a pay raise, or quit and go to work for the competitor. Most important, the capacity of machines often greatly surpasses human capacity.

The frustrations expressed by rural Americans, and others with working-class jobs are real and should be addressed (Cramer 2016; Hochschild 2016). Millions of people throughout rural America are desperate for hope. The critical question is, what is the best way to address these concerns? I recognize the complexity of the issue and that cultural changes and a disappearing way of life are also an important source of rural frustration (Wunthnow 2018) and factors leading to the rise of the "Religious Right" and "Alt-Right" movements (FitzGerald 2017; Neiwert 2017). Addressing the economic concerns, however, seems to be a good place to start.

In my travels in rural America, I often hear from people worried about the direction of change and nostalgic for the past. I understand these worries and fears. A county commissioner once told me that his county had nine sawmills in 1962; the county now has one sawmill. The commissioner told me that if I could help bring back the other eight sawmills, the economic struggles of his county would be over. What everyone associated with rural America needs to understand is that those eight sawmills are not coming back. Chief among reasons for their permanent loss is that one modern sawmill using advanced technology can turn more logs into wood products with fewer workers than all nine sawmills could have done in 1962. The eight missing sawmills are not coming back and neither is the stagecoach, the Pony Express, or the slide rule.

The approach to address the economic concerns of rural America cannot be to return to some golden era of the past. Following my presentation in another rural community, a person approached me and said that people like me were always coming and trying to make their community into something it wasn't. "We have always been a coal-mining town," she told me, "and that is what we should continue to be." My reaction is that the coal industry will never again be what it was and communities that don't want to change are going to be left behind and will soon be nothing but "dust in the wind."

Attempts to return to the golden past will result in our nation falling far behind other countries around the world. Rather, it is essential that we fully embrace the information and service economy and help make rural and blue-collar workers a part of a vibrant twenty-first-century economy. How to accomplish this objective is the goal of this book. To make the necessary changes, it is critical to understand what is happening and why. With this knowledge, it will then be possible to take advantage of potential benefits of the new economy while avoiding many problems and pitfalls.

We would be wise to learn from the massive economic structure transitions resulting from technological changes that have occurred in the past. An obvious example is the Industrial Revolution, beginning in England in the late eighteenth century. This revolution emerged when technological advancements allowed the use of fossil fuels to power new machines. These new machines greatly enhanced human productivity and resulted in many nations transitioning from agricultural-based to industrial-based economies. At times this transition was extremely rocky and resulted in the loss of millions of agricultural and other jobs of that era. Attempts to resist industrial growth, however, would have been futile and counterproductive and would have resulted in the resisting nation falling far behind other nations. While there were rough times during the transition, there were many societal benefits as well. Among the benefits were a higher standard of living, better health, a longer lifespan, and safer and more fulfilling jobs.

The same factors hold true with the current economic structure transformation. Many jobs and skills are becoming obsolete. Of course, this is tremendously difficult for impacted persons and communities. At the same time, new technologies are opening doors for the creation of new jobs, many of which have not yet even been imagined. As will be described in this book, these new economic opportunities can be especially beneficial for rural areas. Additionally, products resulting from the new economy will greatly enhance our standard of living. We can all benefit from access to more information and improved methods of communication. We can benefit as jobs that are dangerous and dull are replaced by jobs that are more interesting and fulfilling. Nations, communities, and individuals can choose to jump aboard and reap the benefits, or they can hide their head in the sand and be left behind as the rest of the world moves forward. If US policy aims to return to a bygone era, our nation will quickly become a second-rate country as the rest of the world advances.

## The Twenty-First-Century Information and Service Economy

The current economic structure transition and its wide-ranging impacts on rural America are primarily a consequence of a variety of new technologies that replace human labor. Especially significant is the proliferation of computers, the Internet, and other forms of information and communication technology. Among the impacts of computers and the Internet are vast amounts of information available at the stroke of a computer key and instantaneous communication with persons anywhere in the world. The benefits of these new technologies to education, medicine, and entertainment are obvious. Businesses benefit from the availability of greater amounts of data and increased capacity to analyze that data.

Computers have also enhanced the capacity of the machines being used in manufacturing and other goods producing industries. As a result, machines used in these industries are even more efficient and thus replace even more human labor in the production process. In today's world, computer-guided machines harvest agricultural crops, milk cows, cut trees, drill for oil, mine coal, and, in the form of robots, operate the machines used in manufacturing. Examples of these machines and their impacts are provided in chapters throughout this book.

Since an economic structure transition was the cause of the current economic malaise in rural America, fully embracing that transition is the key to building a vibrant twenty-first-century economy. Specifically, modern information and communication technology have reduced the relevance of distance and opened doors for rural Americans that simply didn't exist in the past (Albrecht 2014a). Rather than resisting or trying to return to the past, we need to prepare for and take full advantage of opportunities available in the new economy. Specific approaches to accomplishing this objective are described in chapter 10.

## Sources of Rural Economic Disadvantage

Rural America has always been economically disadvantaged relative to urban America. In rural areas, incomes have always been lower, poverty rates higher, and unemployment and underemployment more extensive (Albrecht et al. 2000).

The current economic structure transformation has had even greater implications for rural American than it has for urban America. This is because rural residents have always been more dependent on jobs in the goods producing industries, while urban economies have tended to be much more diverse. Because of their greater dependence on the declining goods producing industries, rural areas did not recover from the Great Recession as quickly or as completely as urban areas (Farrigan 2015; Hertz et al. 2014). In nonmetropolitan counties, the poverty rate has actually increased since the end of the 2007–2009 recession. In contrast, poverty rates have declined significantly in metropolitan areas during the same time period.

Urban economic advantages over rural areas are a consequence of two major factors—location and population size (Albrecht 2012). First, with respect to location, urbanization means that being near markets and suppliers reduces transportation costs. Also, urbanization typically means a larger pool of potential workers, often with industry-specific skills that ensures both a lower probability of unemployment for workers and a lower probability of labor shortages for business (Krugman 1991; Venables 2003). Further, research clearly shows that workers with similar knowledge and skill sets are more productive when working in close proximity and having face-to-face interactions with others than when working in isolation. Interaction and the exchange of ideas resulting from agglomeration greatly enhance creativity (Gaspar and Glaeser 1998; Glaeser 2011; Storper and Venables 2004). Many rural communities exist where they do because their location provides access to a resource (farmland, minerals, forests, etc.) critical for the goods producing industries. These locations may be isolated from urban areas, which has contributed to rural disadvantage.

Population size provides further advantages for urban areas. A larger population provides opportunities for more specialized services and greater economic opportunities. These advantages can be illustrated by looking at health care. Many small towns have a doctor or two and perhaps even a small hospital. However, these small-town doctors are unlikely to be heart surgeons, and the small-town hospital is unlikely to specialize in heart surgery. The population is simply not large enough to provide enough patients with bad hearts to support such specialization. Medical specialists are usually located in large cities, where they draw clientele not only from the larger urban population base but also from surrounding rural areas that do not have that specialized service. The same urban advantage exists in many other industries, including finance, insurance, sports, and politics.

Further, population size provides vast economy of scale advantages. Laying broadband cable to a city where a million inhabitants will subscribe is more profitable than laying broadband to a small community where 200 households will subscribe. The telecoms thus lack motivation to provide adequate Internet to rural areas, and as a consequence rural broadband service is generally not as good (Whitacre et al. 2015). Similarly, urban areas have advantages with respect to many educational technologies and programs. These technologies or programs often have substantial initial cost, whether 10 students or 10,000 students use the technology or program. Thus, per-student costs are lower in urban areas.

The consequence of urban advantage is that the incomes of full-time rural workers are only about 82 percent as high as their urban counterparts when controlling for industry of employment, race/ethnicity, age, and gender. Rural/urban differences increase steadily as education levels increase (Albrecht 2012). For persons with less than a high school degree, rural and urban incomes are virtually identical. Then, as education level increases, the income gap becomes progressively larger. Persons with a postgraduate degree could expect to earn $75,225 in rural areas in 2012. This is only 71.2 percent as much as the $105,618 this person could expect to earn in an urban area.

As will be described in chapter 10, modern technology at least partly reduces these rural disadvantages. By using the computer and Internet, rural residents can market their products to potential consumers throughout the world, thus reducing the problem of a smaller local population. Persons with some specialized skills can market these skills broadly, thus reducing the problems associated with location. Some differences, however, remain. The products of some businesses cannot be marketed effectively to distant consumers; a restaurant is an obvious example. Further, the face-to-face advantages of interaction are not completely offset by online communications.

Thus, at least into the foreseeable future, we can expect that average incomes in urban areas to continue to be higher than in rural areas and that people who chose to live in rural areas will often pay an economic cost.

## Advantages of Rural Living

Many people are willing to forego the economic advantages of urban living for the benefits of living in a rural area. Millions of people in the United States desire to live in rural areas, but traditionally have been unable to do so because of limited job availability (Cromartie 2009; Travis 2007). For those individuals, it is now often possible by using modern information and communication technology to find a way to live in the rural area of their choice.

Among the many benefits of living in rural America are living next to nature where one can quickly be in the mountains or the forest. Many people enjoy nature-based activities such as hiking, nature photography, fishing, hunting, and skiing, and many of these activities are easily accessible to most rural residents. Many people enjoy the close-knit interaction patterns that proliferate in small towns. Others want to remain in their hometown amid friends and family. For many people, living in rural areas means enjoying peace and quiet while avoiding the congestion, crime, and pollution common in urban communities (Wirth 1938). Whatever the reason may be, quality of life can be improved when people live where they wish to, rather than living where their job requires them to be.

## Consequences of Rural Economic Disadvantage and Decline

Finding a way to revitalize the rural economy is extremely important. The serious economic problems that are currently being experienced by the residents of rural America have significant consequences. Most fundamentally, the decline in the number of jobs in the goods producing industries and reduced wages for remaining workers have resulted in the decline of the "Great American Middle Class." The middle-class America of decades past has largely been replaced by a two-tier society, where the divide between the advantaged and disadvantaged is large and becoming ever larger. Most of the economic growth of recent decades has gone to those with already-high incomes (Stiglitz 2012). To be born into one segment of society then crossing the wide chasm to the other side is more and more difficult and increasingly rare (Chetty et al. 2014). As a result, to a growing degree the social class that a person resides in as an adult is determined by the circumstances of their birth. In the America of today, millions of talented and energetic kids with disadvantaged parents have virtually no chance of achieving a lifestyle that those from advantaged families accept as a matter of course. Increasingly, rural Americans are finding themselves on the disadvantaged side of the chasm. This result is very troubling in a nation that has always prided itself in being a land of opportunity, a land where anybody can become anything they want to.

Being born disadvantaged impacts many aspects of life. There is a strong relationship between economic circumstances and health (Berkman and Kawachi 2000). Disadvantaged individuals are less able to afford visits to health care professionals, less likely to have health insurance, and tend to consume a less healthy diet. Poor health reduces performance both at school and in the workforce, which has long-term economic consequences. Recent research, in fact, has found a marked increase in mortality rates among white, middle-aged men and women with lower levels of educational attainment (Case and Deaton 2015). This increased death rate appears especially prominent among rural residents (Snyder 2016). Of special significance in recent years are high rates of opioid addiction and overdose deaths among rural and disadvantaged populations (Monnat and Rigg 2016). There are counties in Appalachia where life expectancy today is less than in 1980 and on par with places such as Ethiopia.

The economically disadvantaged, especially those living in rural areas, also have significantly fewer educational opportunities. Two factors are relevant. First, schools are largely funded by local property taxes. This source of funding means that schools in poor communities have fewer resources than schools in wealthier neighborhoods. Often underfunded schools fail to get young people excited about learning or motivated to continue their education. Second, the rising cost of a college education makes it much more difficult for persons with fewer economic resources to attend and complete college. The subsequent limited education for the disadvantaged means limited employment opportunities, which then puts their children in a position where educational opportunities are subsequently limited, and the cycle continues (Haveman et al. 2001).

There is also a strong relationship between economic disadvantage and crime (Benson et al. 2003; Byrne and Sampson 1986). Living in disadvantaged communities with high crime rates increases the likelihood of being a victim of crime. Additionally, the fear of crime reduces quality of life. Further, many of the costs of economic disadvantage are psychological. Economic hardship means wondering how next month's rent and utility bill will be paid, or even if there will be food on the table. The stress from these concerns results in higher divorce rates and more family problems (Booth and Amato 1991). Moreover, economic disadvantage often leads to a sense of inferiority when interacting with others. The costs of these feelings are impossible to measure.

The cumulative effect of hardship on so many levels is that economically disadvantaged persons tend to experience higher levels of drug addiction, alcoholism, and suicide. Substance abuse is often an attempt to cope with despair (Resnick et al. 1997). Collectively, drug addiction, alcoholism, and suicide have become known as "Diseases of Despair." For example, the opioid epidemic has been especially problematic for persons in rural areas and among blue-collar workers experiencing economic distress. Since 2000, nearly 800,000 people in the United States have died of drug overdoses. The opioid epidemic is especially devastating in economically depressed areas such as Appalachia and struggling "Rust Belt" communities (Haven et al. 2011; Monnat 2018). The subsequent despair and anger from all of these outcomes were apparent in the 2016 election. Clearly, the best way to address the opioid epidemic and other rural problems would be to improve economic conditions.

## Policies to Assist Rural America

In some ways, the current problems being experienced by rural Americans are a consequence of being ignored or forgotten in the policy-making arena in recent decades. At one time, the residents of rural America were a large enough segment of the US population that they exerted a strong political voice. Through the years, the United States has become increasingly urbanized, with rural residents comprising an ever-smaller segment of the population. The result has been a subsequent reduction of their political power (Paarlberg 1980). At both the national and state levels, policy makers have adhered to the wishes of their urban constituents, upon whom they are dependent to win the next election. The lack of concern for rural America has meant that policy makers have not adequately addressed their concerns.

Rural residents have felt betrayed by both political parties. At one time, most blue-collar workers (and thus many workers in the goods producing industries) voted Democrat because of their support for labor unions. In recent decades, membership in labor unions has declined, which has diminished support for Democrats. Most rural residents are hard pressed to find a Democrat policy in recent years that has directly benefitted them. Many feel the Democrat Party's strong emphasis on environmental issues has harmed rural job opportunities in mining, manufacturing, and other goods producing industries.

In recent decades, most rural residents have voted Republican, largely because of the Republican conservative stand on social issues such as abortion and same-sex marriage (Frank 2004; Wunthnow 2018). The resistance of Republicans to social programs benefitting minorities has also played a role in a larger share of white rural residents voting Republican (Hochschild 2016). A number of studies have found that many Americans believe that welfare programs benefit minorities and that these minority individuals lack a strong work ethic and take advantage of the system (Gilens 1999; Quadagno 1994; Wetts and Willer 2018). As was clear from the 2016 election, rural residents have never been totally committed to the Republican philosophy of cutting taxes for the wealthy and then cutting programs for the working class.

Those interested in attaining a greater proportion of the rural vote need to understand the issues and then develop policies that address these issues. I have no question that policies that benefit rural America will also benefit urban Americans as well. Of particular importance, to survive and thrive in a twenty-first-century economy, access to modern information and communication technology is critical. As mentioned earlier, rural America tends to be disadvantaged in this arena compared to urban areas (Whitacre et al. 2015). Closing the digital divide would be a good place for the policy discussion to begin. Other policy suggestions are provided in chapter 10.

## Moving Forward

Making a reality of the changes suggested in this book will not be easy to achieve. Change means doing things differently than they have been done in the past. Change means outdated jobs will become obsolete and will be replaced by new jobs. Change means new skills and training will be required. As such, there will be substantial resistance, at least initially. The alternative, however, is to continue the process of slow, eroding decline that is currently underway.

In this book, I describe my vision for a twenty-first-century economy in rural America. I begin by devoting a chapter to each of several major, traditional goods producing industries, including manufacturing (chapter 1), agriculture (chapter 2), coal (chapter 3), oil and gas (chapter 4), logging (chapter 5), mining (chapter 6), and amenities and tourism (chapter 7). In the next two chapters, federal policies related to the environment (chapter 8) and federal land management (chapter 9) are discussed, as these policies have significant implications for the goods producing industries in rural America. For each chapter, I visit at least one community that has historically been dependent economically on the particular industry or impacted by federal policies. I then examine the resulting consequences of economic change for the community. In the concluding chapter (chapter 10), I outline what a twenty-first-century economy in rural America will look like and how we can achieve it.

I feel qualified to write this book for several reasons. Perhaps most important, I genuinely care about and have deep roots in rural America. I grew up on a farm in a small and isolated rural community. Second, I believe my knowledge and understanding of rural America are unsurpassed. I have spent my entire professional career studying the causes and consequences of economic change in rural America. I have written many other books and articles on this topic. In my current position as director of the Western Rural Development Center, I travel widely and interact extensively with the leaders and residents of rural America. I have listened and learned, and the path that needs to be taken is clear. If we make the right choices, the future of rural America can be very bright indeed.

# 1

# Manufacturing

Manufacturing is the process of turning raw materials into finished or semi-finished products. While manufacturing has always existed, during the Industrial Revolution the process became much more efficient, and the range of products expanded. The Industrial Revolution began in England in the late eighteenth century and was a result of the development of new energy sources and machines that allowed more and better products to be made in a shorter amount of time. An early catalyst for the Industrial Revolution was the development of the steam engine. The steam engine provided a source of energy to power a wide range of newly invented machines.

The first industry to be completely altered by the Industrial Revolution was textiles. Prior to the Industrial Revolution, the process of turning natural fibers such as wool, flax, or cotton into thread or yarn and then into cloth or clothing was a labor-intensive and tedious process and was mostly a home-based or cottage industry. Following the invention of the steam engine, increasingly efficient machines were developed that could do the necessary tasks mechanically. Soon, textile factories emerged with large hired labor

DOI: 10.7330/9781607329510.c001

forces that were vastly more efficient than home production. Additionally, the quality of the clothing produced by factories was typically much better than that from home production. Many rural residents moved to the city to find employment in the emerging factories.

After industrialization of the textile industry, other machines were developed that transformed virtually every other industry and nearly every aspect of human life. The industrialization of agriculture had especially great impacts, since prior to industrialization most people were involved in agriculture. Utilizing new machines, each individual farmer was much more productive and could manage a much larger operation; thus, fewer farmers were needed. As a consequence, many primarily rural and agricultural societies were transformed into urban and industrial societies. Another dramatic consequence of industrialization was the separation of work and family. Prior to industrialization, the family working together at their home did most of the economic production. In effect, the family was both a unit of production and a unit of consumption. After industrialization, the father would typically leave home to work and bring home a paycheck. The mother generally stayed home to care for the children. The family was no longer a unit of production, but rather simply a unit of consumption.

Millions of people were displaced from their jobs by these new industrial machines. Many skilled craftsmen such as cobblers, coopers, and blacksmiths were pushed out of business by industrial production of their products. Yet other jobs emerged to take their place. Most obvious were the new jobs in the manufacturing sector. In addition, with more people freed from the necessity of producing basic food or shelter, many people had opportunities to become skilled in medicine, art, literature, entertainment, and education. With greater levels of production, more people were able to afford these new opportunities. The result was that most people benefitted from these new opportunities, and the quality of life improved greatly for nearly everyone.

The new jobs emerging as a result of the Industrial Revolution required different knowledge and skills and often required people to live in different places. Urban communities generally benefitted, while rural communities struggled. Some people fought hard against the changes. For example, Luddites were a group of English workers who sought to destroy new textile machinery in an effort to prevent the changes they saw as threatening to their way of life. Opposition to change remains common in human communities.

The growing manufacturing sector needed more and more workers. From the outset, there was conflict between this increasingly large labor force and the owners of factories. The workers desired to be paid enough to allow a somewhat comfortable standard of living, to provide opportunities for their children, and to have a safe working environment and reasonable working hours. Ownership desired to keep costs as low as possible, while maximizing production. In many ways, these goals are in direct opposition. For management to provide what labor desired would reduce profits. As the industrial sector grew, relations between labor and management became among the most important concerns of industrial societies. When Karl Marx and Friedrich Engels wrote the *Communist Manifesto* in 1848, their primary purpose was to provide a political system that protected the rights of workers in industrial societies.

The methods and machines of the Industrial Revolution soon crossed the Atlantic from Britain to America. Most Americans embraced industrialization, and in time the United States became the most advanced industrialized country in the world. Throughout the nineteenth century, rapid developments occurred in industries such as steel and oil production. Railroads were built from one end of the country to the other, making it possible for the inputs and products of the growing industrial sector to get transported quickly and with greater cost effectiveness. Early manufacturing was concentrated in the northeastern quadrant of the country, largely because of access to a labor force and sources of energy.

In time a large textile-manufacturing sector emerged, primarily in the South. By the close of World War II, 1.3 million Americans were employed in textile and apparel manufacturing. At this time, about 40 percent of the North Carolina labor force was employed in the textile sector. Textile manufacturing in the South tended to pay lower wages than the heavy manufacturing occurring in northern and eastern states.

Labor disputes soon became prominent in the US industrial sector. In most early labor disputes, government officials and law enforcement tended to side with management and ownership. On a number of occasions in the late eighteenth and early nineteenth centuries, industries hired private security agencies, such as the Pinkerton Agency, a private detective service, to infiltrate unions and intimidate workers. In several cases, conflicts between labor and management resulted in injuries and death. In the Great Strike of 1877, more than 100 people were killed. The Homestead Strike of 1892 was a conflict between the steel workers and management at a Carnegie Steel Company plant in Homestead, near Pittsburgh, Pennsylvania. Ownership brought in the Pinkertons, and battles between the workers and the Pinkertons resulted in the deaths of at least a dozen people. Numerous other labor conflicts occurred in a wide range of locations.

In the years immediately following World War II, the US manufacturing sector embarked on a period of spectacular growth. Utilizing continually improving technologies, American manufacturers were able to produce a wide range of products quite cheaply, and then market these products throughout the world. Innovation was aided by public investment in basic research at universities that resulted in new products, techniques, and ideas. Advanced industrialization resulted in high productivity, which led to high profits. Under these circumstances, unions were able to seek and obtain higher wages for their workers. This progress resulted in the historically unique situation in which ordinary workers were earning relatively high incomes (Bluestone and Harrison 1982; Chevan and Stokes 2000; Danziger and Gottschalk 1995; Sassen 1990).

With millions of well-paying jobs in manufacturing, the United States was very much a middle-class nation in the decades following World War II. Persons getting a manufacturing job could generally afford a home, a car, a family vacation, and, if they wished, send their children to college. Through these decades there was a steadily improving standard of living, with each generation doing measurably better economically than their parents. Between the end of World War II and 1973, real wages doubled for the average American worker. It was a time of optimism, with most people expecting economic growth to continue (Brick 1998; Uslaner 1998). In his much-acclaimed book *The Affluent Society*, the well-known economist John Kenneth Galbraith (1958) wrote that greater production would result in economic prosperity reaching nearly all Americans and that only "pockets" of poverty would remain.

While manufacturing occurred throughout the country, the Upper Midwest and Northeast became the most industrialized region of the country. Nearly all cities in this region had substantial manufacturing enterprises. Some cities became known for their primary product. For example, the auto industry was centered in Detroit, Pittsburgh was the steel city, and tires were manufactured in Akron, Ohio.

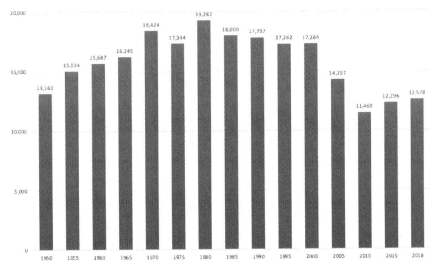

**FIGURE 1.1.** Manufacturing employment in the United States (in thousands), 1950–2018

Initially, most US manufacturing occurred in urban areas. In time, some industrial firms began moving to rural areas in an attempt to pay lower wages to their workers. In rural areas, industry could employ farmworkers displaced by improving technology and seek to avoid unionization. The wages one could earn in manufacturing generally far exceeded what could be earned in farming, thus it was relatively easy to attract the necessary workforce. Soon manufacturing employment far exceeded farm employment, even in rural areas, and the proportional dependence of rural areas on manufacturing exceeded that of urban areas (Low 2017). Communities that could obtain an industrial firm often had the benefit of an employer that paid relatively high wages and employed workers that lacked an advanced education. During this era, community economic development often consisted of attempting to attract an industrial firm to operate there.

Employment in manufacturing continued to grow until reaching a peak in 1979, with more than 19.5 million employees (figure 1.1). Since that time, there has been a somewhat steady decline in manufacturing employment. Declines were especially pronounced from 2000 to about 2010. In 2018, the number employed in the manufacturing sector was down to about 12.6 million, a

55 percent decline from 1979. There has been a small rebound since 2010, as the economy recovers from the 2008 recession. As the number of jobs declined, there was not a corresponding decline in the number of people seeking these jobs. As a result, management was able to pay lower wages for unskilled workers and reduce the power of the unions (Kingsolver 1989; Rosenblum 1995). Consequently, the power of unions today is much reduced, and the proportion of workers belonging to a union is much lower compared to the decades immediately following World War II.

While some industries moved to countries with lower wages and less-restrictive environmental regulations, the vast majority of jobs lost in manufacturing are a consequence of technological developments whereby machines replace human labor in the production process (Hicks and Devaraj 2015; Rasker 2017). Thus, even though employment numbers are down, the value of production from manufacturing continues to grow. In fact, the value of goods produced in manufacturing in the United States has doubled since the 1980s. With improved technology, a small number of workers can produce more than a much larger workforce in times past.

The greater reliance on technology also means that the modern manufacturing sector requires workers with more skills and higher levels of education. Between 2000 and 2014, the proportion of manufacturing employees with at least a bachelor's degree increased from 22 percent to 29 percent. No question, this trend will continue and the capacity of manufacturing to provide jobs to unskilled workers will diminish. A more educated and skilled workforce also means that average wages in the manufacturing sector have increased and likely will continue to increase. In contrast, wages continue to fall for the declining number of unskilled workers.

It is also important to understand that manufacturing is not a monolithic industry and that some sectors of that industry have done better than others. The skills needed and wages paid also vary by manufacturing sector. For example, between 2002 and 2012, motor vehicle parts manufacturing lost 254,000 jobs, which was 53 percent of that industry's labor force. During this same time period, household and institutional furniture manufacturing lost 185,900 jobs, which was 85 percent of their labor force. In the South between 1997 and 2009, 650 textile-manufacturing plants closed, with thousands of workers being laid off. The plants that remain are more automated, require a smaller but more skilled labor force, and are more productive than plants that existed in the past.

In rural areas, the most important manufacturing sector is food manu-facturing. Wood manufacturing is also heavily concentrated in rural areas. For both of these sectors, there are advantages for manufacturing firms of being near the resource (agricultural products or trees). Employment in food manufacturing has remained relatively constant and without the drastic job losses experienced by other sectors. Wood manufacturing has not been so fortunate, as there has been substantial job loss. In rural areas, the largest employment declines have been in textile and apparel manufacturing.

## Manufacturing's Decline

The manufacturing proportion of US GDP has been declining as other sectors of the US economy continue to grow. In 1958, manufacturing's share of the GDP reached a peak at 28 percent. Between 2001 and 2015, the proportional share of the GDP from manufacturing declined from 14 percent to 12 percent.

With the number of jobs declining and plants closing since about 1980, the Upper Midwest region became known as the "Rust Belt." The implications of declining employment in manufacturing were dramatic, as many cities lost the most important sector of their economy. Of the many cities that could be used as an example of the consequences of deindustrialization, Youngstown, Ohio, and Flint, Michigan, are often considered the poster children.

*Youngstown, Ohio*

Around the turn of the twentieth century, Youngstown became one of the most important steel-producing cities in the country. By 1930, steel mills lined the Mahoning River for miles and the population of Mahoning County (where Youngstown is located) grew from 55,979 in 1890 to 236,142 in 1930 and then to 303,424 in 1970. With thousands of well-paying jobs in the steel industry, the city was prospering.

The decline of the steel industry in Youngstown began on September 19, 1977, a day remembered locally as "Black Monday." On that day, 5,000 workers were laid off without warning when they arrived at work. The loss of jobs continued through the 1980s as more steel mills closed. Some plants began to mechanize in an attempt to remain profitable, which resulted in

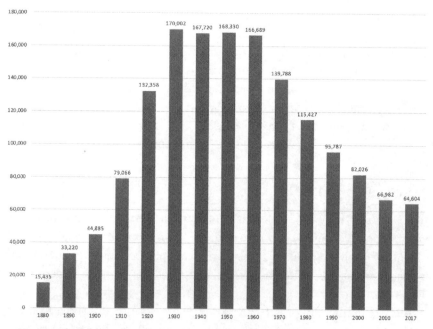

**FIGURE 1.2.** Population trends in Youngstown, Ohio, 1880–2017

the loss of even more jobs. Overall, more than 50,000 jobs in the steel indus-try were lost in the county, and the steel industry has largely disappeared. The massive steel factories are now nothing more than rusting hulks. With thousands of jobs disappearing, large numbers of people moved away. Those who remained are living in a city plagued by crime, drugs, and deteriorating schools and infrastructure.

According to US Census data, between 2010 and 2016, Youngstown had the highest rate of population decline and the highest poverty rate among the 100 largest metropolitan areas in the country. By 2016, the population of Mahoning County was down to 230,008, a 32 percent decline from 1970. The city of Youngstown has done even worse than the rest of Mahoning County. In 1930, the city's population was 170,002; in 2017 this number had been reduced to 64,604 (figure 1.2). Journalist Chris Hedges stated that Youngstown is "a deserted wreck plagued by crime and the attendant psycho-logical and criminal problems that come when communities physically break down" (Hedges 2010).

*Flint, Michigan*

The year 1908 marks the formation of the General Motors Company in Flint, Michigan. In the decades to follow, some of GM's most important manufacturing plants were located in Flint. The Flint Sit-Down Strike of 1936–1937 was instrumental in the formation of the United Auto Workers and the growing power of unions. Following World War II, GM's Buick and Chevrolet divisions were centered in Flint. Flint residents referred to their home as "Vehicle City." By the 1960s and 1970s, GM employed about 80,000 workers in their Flint plants. As the need for workers in the auto industry grew, the city grew as well. When GM employment reached its peak, the population of Flint approached 200,000. In the decades after World War II, Flint was an example of a prosperous manufacturing city with a strong working class.

Problems for Flint began in the 1980s as employment in the auto industry began to decline. Of prime significance were technological developments whereby machines replaced human labor in production. Often it was more efficient to build a new plant in another location that was equipped with new technology than to attempt to remodel older plants such as those in Flint. Increased competition from automakers in other countries (such as Japan) was also an important factor. Between 1980 and 2010, the number of GM employees in Flint fell to 8,000, a 90 percent decline.

No community can experience a 90 percent decline in the number of jobs held by their most significant employer without severe negative consequences, and the consequences in Flint were severe. To begin with, the population began a rapid decline, as people moved elsewhere—seeking employment. By 2017, Flint's population was under 100,000, less than one-half of what it had been a few decades earlier (figure 1.3). Another predictable outcome was growing levels of poverty. In 2017, the poverty rate in Flint exceeded 40 percent. Under these circumstances, it is not surprising that the community struggles with high crime rates.

Beginning in 2014, Flint received national attention when the city's water supply was found to have dangerously high levels of lead and other contaminants (Clark 2018). Ten deaths from Legionnaires' disease have been traced to the contaminated water. The problems began when the city changed water supplies in an attempt to save money. At the same time, the city's infrastructure was old and worn and hadn't been updated because the city was so

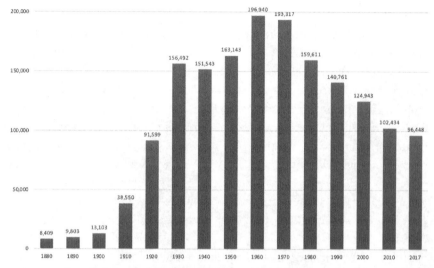

**FIGURE 1.3.** Population trends in Flint, Michigan, 1880–2017

poor. Complaints by Flint residents about discolored, foul-smelling, and bad-tasting water were discounted. Local and state officials didn't seem to consider the complaints credible from Flint residents who were mostly African American and poor. An additional problem was that as the city's population declined, the water system was much too large for the population it was serving. Under these circumstances, the flaking of lead from the aging pipes is more likely. As I am writing this paragraph, Flint residents are still encouraged to drink bottled water.

In other cities, the problems resulting from reduced manufacturing employment are similar. In his classic books on the Chicago inner city, William Julius Wilson (1987, 1996) described the problems that occurred when manufacturing plants closed and jobs disappeared. Of vital importance was the decline of family stability. The stress on marriages that suffer from the lack of a stable income is substantial. Further, women (in particular) are unwilling to marry a man who doesn't have a stable income. Thus, as jobs disappear, the proportion of married adults declines and the proportion of children living in single-parent families increases. Similarly, the crack cocaine epidemic of the 1980s can be tied to the economic struggles resulting from declines in industrial employment.

Deindustrialization has also impacted rural America. Since 2000, the number of jobs in manufacturing in rural America has declined by 30 percent (Low 2017). A smaller plant closing in a rural community usually doesn't get the media attention allotted to the decline of the auto industry in Detroit or Flint or to the death of the steel industry in Pittsburgh or Youngstown. The implications for the small community, however, can be even more devastating. In urban areas, there are often multiple major employers, and the closure of one factory can sometimes be somewhat offset by the presence of others. In contrast, many rural communities are heavily dependent on a single employer. The loss of this one industry can be economically devastating.

## Manufacturing in Wisconsin

Experiences in Wisconsin have mirrored other states in the Upper Midwest. Since settlement, Wisconsin has been and continues to be an important agricultural state, being best known for its dairy industry. It is, however, an even more important manufacturing state. Manufacturing was initially centered in larger cities in Wisconsin such as Milwaukee, and in time spread to many smaller communities as well. As an indication of the significance of manufacturing, at present Wisconsin has a higher proportion of their labor force working in manufacturing (16.3 percent) than any other state in the nation except Indiana. In comparison, fewer than 1 percent of Wisconsin workers are employed in agriculture.

As in other parts of the country, manufacturing employment in Wisconsin has declined substantially since about 1980. In 2000, there were 598,800 manufacturing employees in Wisconsin. During the recession, this number decreased to 423,600. In recent years, some rebound has occurred and in 2017 the number of employees was up to 480,000, which is still a 20 percent decline from 2000.

Milwaukee is Wisconsin's largest city and most important manufacturing center. In Milwaukee, Allis-Chalmers was once the city's most important manufacturing firm. Allis-Chalmers built large-scale farm and construction equipment. In the decades following World War II, Allis-Chalmers employed more than 20,000 people and was the most important employer in all of Milwaukee.

Like industrial plants all over the country, circumstances made a turn for the worse in the 1980s. An important factor for Allis-Chalmers was the dramatic reduction in the number of farms, meaning fewer potential customers for their products. In addition, their competitors were becoming more efficient, a change that reduced their profit margin. In an attempt to remain competitive, Allis-Chalmers began to lay off employees during the 1980s and to use more efficient technology, which replaced even more workers. These efforts failed, and in 1987 Allis-Chalmers was forced to declare bankruptcy. In 1999, the last company office in Milwaukee was closed. The vast Allis-Chalmers manufacturing site has become a wasteland. Pockets of the area are now used as parking lots and a shopping center. The subsequent high levels of unemployment and underemployment in the city have resulted in severe social and economic problems (Desmond 2016).

In other cities around the state, smaller industries have met the same fate as Allis-Chalmers. While the total number of employees in these industries is not as large, the implications for the smaller communities are equally devastating. Janesville, Wisconsin, is located between Madison and Chicago in southern Wisconsin. In 1919, General Motors opened an assembly plant in Janesville. This plant produced their first Chevrolet on Valentine's Day 1923 (Goldstein 2017). For decades, the Janesville Assembly Plant produced thousands of vehicles and was the most important employer in the city. Employment levels reached a peak in 1970, with about 7,000 workers at the Janesville Assembly Plant. Since then, employment numbers steadily declined, primarily as a result of improved mechanization. By 2008, the number of employees had been reduced to about 1,200. Then on December 23, 2008, the plant produced its last vehicle, a Chevrolet Tahoe. The doors to the plant were then locked and all of the workers were out of a job. Until that time, the Janesville Assembly Plant was the longest operating GM plant in the world. As can be imagined, the consequences for the individuals involved and for the City of Janesville were devastating (Goldstein 2017).

The process of deindustrialization continues. In early 2018, Kimberly-Clark, the makers of Kleenex and Huggies diapers, announced that they were closing several plants and 5,000 workers will be laid off. Many of the lost jobs are in Wisconsin.

Richland Center provides another example of manufacturing decline in a rural Wisconsin community.

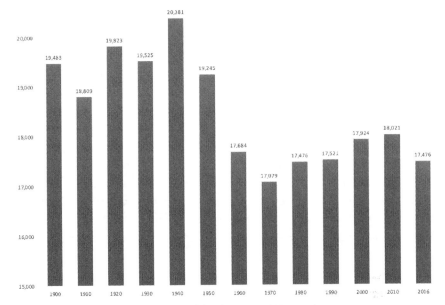

**FIGURE 1.4.** Population trends in Richland County, Wisconsin

*Richland Center, Wisconsin*

Richland Center is located about sixty miles west of Madison, the state capitol and the state's second largest city. The drive from Madison to Richland Center on a summer day allows one to enjoy views of cornfields, dairy cows grazing, and rolling green hills, a picture of rural tranquility. In 2016, the population of Richland County (where Richland Center is located) was 17,476, a decline from the county's population peak of 20,381 reached in 1940 (figure 1.4). Most early settlers to the area were involved in agriculture, and agriculture remains significant in the region as is apparent when driving around Richland County. Much of the population decline during the middle decades of the twentieth century was a consequence of the industrialization of agriculture.

Like many other smaller communities in the Upper Midwest, Richland Center was able to successfully attract industrial firms, mostly during the middle decades of the twentieth century. Manufacturing employment offset the loss of jobs in agriculture and provided many solid, middle-income jobs that brought economic stability and vibrancy to the community. Young people who were no longer needed in agriculture could find a manufacturing job and thus didn't have to leave home. Not surprisingly in a major dairy producing area like Richland County, the manufacturing of dairy products such as cheese, butter, and yogurt represent a significant part of the manufacturing economy. Several other manufacturing enterprises were located in the county as well. Among the more significant companies, Rockwell Automation builds low-voltage motor control devices and Richland Foundry makes iron castings.

The experiences of Richland Foundry are typical of manufacturing firms throughout the country. Richland Foundry began operation in 1963. By the early 2000s, the Foundry employed 275 people and was the single-most-important employer in Richland County. Periodically, during the next several years, some of the employees were laid off as profit margins declined. Then on Friday, December 4, 2015, seventy-four foundry employees were met at the door and told not to return to work the following Monday morning. This move was prompted by the foundry's decision to declare bankruptcy. The action was obviously devastating for the persons involved, as there was no warning and the layoffs occurred just before Christmas. The loss of so many good jobs was also destructive for the entire community. The stability and vibrancy that had existed in Richland Center were quickly evaporating.

Tom Johnson (not his real name) was one of the people who lost his job on that cold December day in 2015. Because he was the primary wage earner of his family (his wife and four kids), the financial blow was severe. Tom's specialized industrial skill set (which included an engineering degree from the University of Wisconsin) meant that available jobs that would pay anything close to what he had been earning were rare, especially in a small town such as Richland Center. The family didn't want to move to find another job, as the kids were integrated into their schools and activities and his wife had a part-time job that she enjoyed and whose income helped the family financially. As the months went by, Tom was forced to expand his job search to throughout Wisconsin and eventually to neighboring states, but was still unable to find a job.

Several months later, Tom was invited to return to Richland Foundry. Following bankruptcy, the company had reorganized and reopened for business. The newly restructured operation was much more dependent on machines and technologies than it had been previously. While once employing

275 people, Richland Foundry now has 27 employees. As is the case with so many other operations, despite having only 10 percent as many employees compared to previous decades, Richland Foundry production has not declined. Increased production, however, is little consolation to the scores of people who have lost their jobs. A critical factor in Tom being asked to return is the fact that he has a degree in engineering. His skills and knowledge will be helpful in the foundry as it is now highly automated. People lacking specialized skills were not invited to return when the plant reopened, and people without such skills are unlikely to find employment there in the future.

Declining employment in manufacturing played a vital role in the 2016 presidential election. Disgruntled voters who had seen their jobs disappear were drawn to the message of Donald Trump. He promised to bring back manufacturing jobs by reducing immigration, changing trade agreements, and implementing tariffs. These promises were enough to turn to his side rural voters in key swing states such as Wisconsin, Michigan, and Pennsylvania. President Obama had won these three states in both 2008 and 2012. As a result of the rural vote, Trump was able to win a very close election in all three states, which sealed his win. Obama was victorious is Richland County in both 2008 and 2012, while Richland County voters went for Trump in 2016.

## Conclusions

Manufacturing will remain a significant segment of the US economy in the years and decades to come. Manufacturing employment numbers, however, will never again approach what they were in the past. Trends toward machines replacing human labor in the production process will continue, and fewer workers will be able to produce even more. While manufacturing can remain an important aspect of a community's economy, it is essential that communities that are heavily dependent on manufacturing find a way to diversify, as total employment in manufacturing is likely to continue to decline. The skill levels required in the manufacturing sector will continue to grow. Renegotiating trade agreements, implementing tariffs, and limiting immigration will have little impact on these trends. Community economic development strategy needs to move beyond seeking to attract an industrial enterprise. As will be described in chapter 10, becoming a part of the twenty-first-century economy will be an important step in the right direction.

# 2

# Agriculture

European immigrants to America in the early 1600s brought with them a form of agriculture that was primitive by modern standards. Utilizing farming techniques of the day, most families were unable to produce much more than what was needed for household consumption, and thus there was little surplus for the marketplace. Since we all must eat, by necessity virtually everyone was involved in agriculture. When the first US Census was taken in 1790, 96 percent of US residents were rural. Although farmers were not enumerated separately, it is believed that nearly all rural residents at the time were involved in farming to some degree (Albrecht and Murdock 1990).

After the formation of the United States, the opportunity to farm one's own land was the magnet that lured many landless and land-hungry European settlers to the United States and later pulled them westward across the country (Cochrane 1979). The privilege to own land was enshrined in the Declaration of Independence and the Bill of Rights, and was the historical basis for US farm policy, which emphasized getting land into the hands of individuals and

DOI: 10.7330/9781607329510.c002

families. The Homestead Act of 1862 perhaps best symbolized the American ideal of providing land to those desiring to farm and seeking to establish a system of medium-sized, owner-occupied farms throughout the country. After laying claim to 160 acres and paying a small registration fee, an individual could gain clear ownership of this land after five years by living on the land and making improvements.

As the country expanded westward, the number of farms increased as greater amounts of land were brought into production. Where soil was more productive or rainfall sufficient and consistent, the density of farms was greater. Where water or other resources were lacking, tremendous effort was made to provide irrigation or other resources to make agriculture possible or to increase its productivity. The expansion of agriculture resulted in thousands of communities emerging throughout the country to provide services to farmers and their families.

Through the years, gradual improvements in farm technology occurred allowing increased productivity and a reduction in the amount of farm labor required. Subsequently, a smaller proportion of the population was needed in agriculture as many farm families could now produce an ever-growing surplus. By 1910, farms had been established throughout the country, and the number of farms exceeded 6 million. At this time, the farm population surpassed 30 million people, which was about one-third of the total US population. The number of farms and the farm population then remained virtually unchanged for the next 30 years until about 1940. Through these years, as the nation's total population grew, farmers obviously became a smaller proportion of the total population. In 1940, less than one-fourth of the US population was involved in agriculture.

Since 1940 rapid change has occurred in US agriculture. Continually improving technology has allowed machines to replace human labor in the production process. For example, in 1930 over 23 billion hours of farm labor were required in the United States; by 2012 only 2.5 billion hours of labor were required. With machines doing more of the work, it became possible for an individual farmer to operate many times the number of acres his predecessors could operate (Paarlberg 1980). As a result, by the 1980s, the number of farms in the country was down to only 2.2 million and the farm population had dropped from 30 million to barely 5 million. By 1990, the farm population was less than 2 percent of the total population (figure 2.1),

**TABLE 2.1.** Changes in Farm Structure, 1900–2012

| Year | Number of Farms (1,000) | Average Farm Size (Acres) |
|------|------------------------|---------------------------|
| 1900 | 5,740 | 147 |
| 1910 | 6,366 | 139 |
| 1920 | 6,454 | 149 |
| 1930 | 6,295 | 157 |
| 1940 | 6,102 | 175 |
| 1950 | 5,388 | 216 |
| 1959 | 3,711 | 303 |
| 1969 | 2,730 | 390 |
| 1982 | 2,241 | 440 |
| 1992 | 1,925 | 491 |
| 2002 | 2,129 | 441 |
| 2012 | 2,109 | 434 |

Source: US Census of Agriculture.

and the US Census quit counting the farm population separately as farmers' numbers had become so small.

I have memories of throwing bales of hay onto a wagon, and sitting on a stool milking cows by hand, squirting the milk into a bucket. Many people in the South have memories of picking cotton by hand. Residents of other parts of the country have similar memories of farm work. Machines now harvest grain, potatoes, and most fruits and vegetables, and they milk cows. Many of the farm jobs that have been replaced by machines were physically challenging and often incredibly dull and monotonous. Vast numbers of agricultural jobs are gone forever, and few who performed this work are mourning their loss.

In addition, chemical fertilizers and pesticides, hybrid seeds, and improved genetics have greatly increased productivity. Thus, not only did the number of acres that an individual farmer could operate increase, but productivity per acre and per animal rose as well. In 1930, on average about twenty bushels of corn were produced per acre in the United States; by 2016, this number had increased to 171. Likewise, the pounds of milk produced per cow per year grew from 5,314 in 1950 to 22,393 in 2015. As a result, the number of people fed by one American farm increased from 7 in 1900 to 155 in 2010 (figure 2.2).

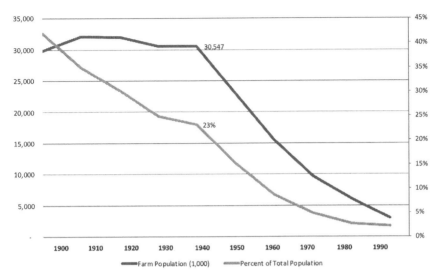

**FIGURE 2.1.** Farm population and percent of total population (in thousands), 1900–1990

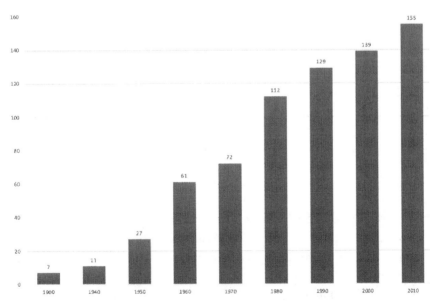

**FIGURE 2.2.** Number of people fed by a single US farmer

Additionally, farmers no longer have to devote a significant proportion of the land to produce feed for work animals such as horses and oxen. Tractors and other machines have replaced work animals.

During most of the twentieth century, when a farmer retired, a neighbor often purchased his or her farm, since this neighbor now had the capacity to operate a much greater acreage using modern machines. As a result, there was one fewer farm and the existing farm was larger. With fewer opportunities in agriculture, young people would often complete high school and move to the city to obtain employment or attend college, never to permanently return to their small-town home. Farm population reductions also resulted from farm families having fewer children. With a smaller farm population, the businesses providing services to farmers and their families in rural communities began to suffer as well. This problem was exacerbated as improved cars and highways made it possible for rural residents to do more of their shopping and other activities in the city. Thus, many rural businesses were forced to close. With fewer farmers and fewer businesses, there was a steadily declining population in hundreds of farm-dependent rural communities throughout the country. In large numbers of communities, the population in 1970 was less than one-half of what it had been in 1940 (Albrecht and Murdock 1990).

While the farm population plummeted, employment in the manufacturing sector surged as described in chapter 1. At the close of World War II, the US industrial sector experienced major growth: technological developments increased our capacity to produce higher-quality products in greater quantities and then to market these products worldwide. Employment in the manufacturing sector increased, as large numbers of displaced farmworkers migrated to the city to seek employment in industry. This option was even more attractive because wages in industry were often much better than in agriculture.

Eventually, the manufacturing sector began moving to rural areas to employ displaced farmworkers, avoid unionization, and keep labor costs down. Soon manufacturing replaced agriculture and the natural resource industries as the primary employer of rural Americans (Albrecht 2014a). Many rural communities that successfully attracted an industrial firm had the benefit of well-paying jobs and demographic stability. Unfortunately, however, communities were not on equal footing in their ability to attract industry. Generally, communities most effective in attracting industry were those that were initially larger, near urban areas, and on major transportation routes (Fuguitt et al. 1989; Johansen and Fuguitt 1984). Many of the smaller and more isolated communities were unable to attract industry. If these communities were farm dependent, they most likely continued their economic and demographic slide.

A nation of medium-sized family farms is a description that no longer fits the United States. Since the 1980s, the total number of farms has stabilized at just over 2 million. In 2012, this number was 2.1 million. Today, however, a large proportion of these farms are part-time and hobby operations that produce only a small share of our food and fiber. In 2012, 81.4 percent of US farms had sales of less than $100,000. These farms, however, generated only 5.4 percent of total farm sales. In contrast, only 3.8 percent of farms had sales exceeding $1 million. These farms, however, had 66.4 percent of total farm sales. Currently, the small family farm accounts for 90 percent of all farms and manages 50 percent of farmland but produces only 23 percent of farm output. The vast majority of household income for the smaller farms comes from nonfarm sources. In fact, only 17 percent of the total household income of all farm families comes from agriculture, with the remaining 83 percent coming from off-farm sources (Fernandez-Cornejo 2007). Thus, most of the food and fiber produced in this country comes from a small number of large commercial farms using advanced technology.

At one point, policy makers argued that having a viable farm sector was essential for the economic health of rural communities. This relationship has now largely reversed. Since most farms are dependent on off-farm income, the survival of these farms requires an economically viable rural community that can provide off-farm jobs to members of the farm family and that allows the family to remain in agriculture. Without off-farm jobs, many farms are unlikely to survive. Those that do survive without off-farm earnings tend to be sufficiently large to allow the family to earn a livable income from farming alone.

To better understand the relationship between agricultural change and community economic development, this chapter examines two counties that have traditionally been very economically dependent on agriculture. Both of these counties are in the Great Plains, a vast area that remains more dependent on agriculture than does the remainder of the country. Many of the more remote areas of the Great Plains have been unable to attract industry to replace declining farm numbers. These counties also lack the high-quality amenities that have been related to economic and demographic growth in recent years. Consequently, the long-term trend has been demographic and economic decline (Johnson and Lichter 2019). The first of the counties to be examined is Daniels County in eastern Montana in the northern Great Plains, while the second is Baca County in eastern Colorado in the southern Great Plains.

## The Great Plains

The Great Plains is a vast region in the middle of the North American continent that is over 2,000 miles long and about 500 miles wide. In his classic 1931 book, Walter Prescott Webb defined the Great Plains as (1) a comparatively flat area, (2) largely treeless and traditionally covered with grass, and (3) often having rainfall insufficient for many traditional forms of agriculture. Definitions vary about precisely where the plains begin and end, but most maintain that the Great Plains begins near the Rio Grande River at the Mexican border in Texas and goes north well into Canada. The Great Plains comprise parts of ten US states, including Texas, New Mexico, Colorado, Oklahoma, Kansas, Nebraska, Wyoming, Montana, South Dakota, and North Dakota. The region also includes parts of three Canadian provinces: Alberta, Manitoba, and Saskatchewan.

For the entire length of the Great Plains, as one travels from east to west, the elevation increases gradually while rainfall diminishes. As a consequence, the eastern portion of the region is a tall-grass prairie, while the western portion is a short-grass prairie. These differences result from variations in rainfall. The 100th meridian has traditionally been recognized as the boundary between the two prairie regions. West of the 100th meridian has generally been considered as lacking sufficient rainfall for most types of farming without irrigation. The 100th meridian cuts through the middle of the Dakotas, Nebraska, and Kansas and then forms the boundary between the Texas Panhandle and Oklahoma. Thus, both the Texas Panhandle and the Oklahoma Panhandle are part of the short-grass prairie.

At one time, vast herds of bison, numbering in the tens of millions, roamed the Great Plains. Other plains fauna includes prairie dogs, deer, rabbits, pronghorns, and their predators such as wolves, coyotes, foxes, and ferrets. The earliest human inhabitants of the Great Plains were a variety of American Indian tribes who lived on the Great Plains for millennia. The lives of persons in these tribes were changed dramatically when they acquired horses initially brought to the Americas by the Spanish. Utilizing horses greatly improved the capacity of Plains Indians to hunt bison and resist the efforts of those attempting to move them from their land. The first people of European ancestry to view the Great Plains were explorers such as Lewis and Clark and fur traders. When settlers began moving to the West Coast, the Great Plains area was labeled as the "great American desert" and was viewed simply as a region to be passed over as quickly as possible to reach what was considered the more desirable West Coast.

Following the Civil War, the vast herds of bison were slaughtered for their hides, to subdue the Plains Indians or simply for sport. The loss of bison crushed the Plains tribes, and they were then forced onto reservations. With bison and Indians removed, people began to examine the economic potential of the Great Plains. The first option was agriculture. Attempts to farm the Great Plains initially occurred in eastern portions of the region, where precipitation levels are greater and more dependable. It became widely accepted that livestock grazing was the most productive use of much of the western or short-grass prairie portion of the Great Plains. After the Civil War, vast numbers of cattle were turned lose on publicly owned lands of the western prairies. The livestock industry was enhanced by high prices for beef resulting from growing demand from eastern industrial centers and the expansion of the railroad that made getting the cattle to marker easier. With high prices and virtually no control over the number of livestock allowed on the publicly owned prairies, the number of livestock grazing on these rangelands soon greatly exceeded capacity. After years of overgrazing, a period of fortunate weather came to a crashing halt with the bitterly cold winter of 1886–1887. Vast numbers of cattle starved to death, and many more malnourished and weakened cattle froze in the vicious cold. Without a way to feed their cattle, ranchers took many more emaciated animals to market, causing prices to collapse (Wilkinson 1992). Future US president Theodore Roosevelt's effort at ranching in North Dakota came to a sudden end during the winter of 1886–1887.

In time, a growing number of farmers pushed slowly westward from the tall-grass prairie region to the drier short-grass prairie regions. The "Enlarged Homestead Act" of 1909, which allowed settlers to claim 320 acres rather than the traditional 160 acres, encouraged this process. The larger acreage was based on the recognition that a greater area was needed to earn a living in a less-productive region of the country. In the latter decades of the nineteenth century and early decades of the twentieth century, thousands of settlers moved to the Great Plains to claim the free land with hopes of making a living from farming. Between 1870 and 1930, about 100 million acres of grassland was plowed and turned into cropland (Cunfer 2005). The implications were extensive, as will be apparent in the two example counties.

The further west settlers moved, the more severe a constraint the lack of water became. After years of ample rainfall, periods of drought would return. Concerning this cycle of boom and bust, the 1896 Yearbook of Agriculture stated:

> The Great Plains can be characterized as a region of periodical famine . . .
> Year after year the water supply may be ample, the forage plants cover the
> ground with rank growth, the herds multiply, the settlers extend their fields,
> when, almost imperceptibly, the climate becomes less humid, the rain clouds
> forming day after day disappear upon the horizon, and weeks lengthen into
> months without a drop of moisture. The grasses wither, the herds wander
> wearily over the plains in search of water holes, the crops wilt and languish,
> yielding not even the seed for another year . . . Another and perhaps another
> season of drought occurs, the settlers depart with such of their household
> furniture as can be drawn away by the enfeebled draft animals, the herds
> disappear, and this beautiful land, once so fruitful, is now dry and brown and
> given over to the prairie wolf. Then comes a season of ample rains. The prai-
> rie grasses, dormant through several seasons, spring into life, and with these
> the hopes of the new pioneers. Then recurs the flood of immigration, to be
> continued until the next long drought. (Newell 1896: 168–169)

To cope with reduced precipitation, attempts to irrigate have been attempted where a water supply is available. Prominently, water pumped from the Ogallala Aquifer, which underlies much of the region, has increased agricultural production on thousands of acres throughout the Great Plains.

## Daniels County, Montana

Daniels County, Montana, is on the Canadian border in eastern Montana. If definitions based on population size and distance from urban areas are used, Daniels County can be classified as the most rural county in the continental United States. It is 340 miles from Scobey, the county seat of Daniels County to Billings, Montana, the nearest metropolitan area. It is 125 miles from Scobey to Williston, North Dakota, the nearest community of any size.

For centuries, vast herds of bison roamed the near treeless rolling plains of the great American prairie of which Daniels County is a part. Following the removal of both bison and American Indians, thousands of cattle were turned lose to graze on this land that at the time was publicly owned. Eventually, a few hardy settlers moved to the area claiming their homestead. Since there was a near total lack of trees, many of the early homes were made of sod with dirt floors. Following the few early settlers, large numbers of homesteaders moved to the Daniels County area in the late 1800s and the first decades of the twentieth century. The climate of the rolling plains of northeast Montana placed significant restrictions on the type of agriculture that could be practiced. Rainfall is inadequate for some crops, and the short growing season that exists on the Canadian border eliminates the possibility for other types of farming. From initial settlement, dryland wheat and cattle grazing on the vast grasslands were the primary agricultural enterprises.

The number of acres devoted to wheat production increased dramatically with the onset of World War I, when the price of wheat skyrocketed. This major increase was primarily because the war in Europe greatly reduced the flow of grain from Russia to Western Europe and efforts were made to have wheat imports from America make up the shortfall. With high wheat prices, many more families moved to the plains to obtain free land and attempt to make a living by farming.

By 1920, the population was adequate for the formation of Daniels County. At that time, there were more than 1,000 farms in the county. With high wheat prices, these farms and the families operating them were doing quite well financially. Then, with the onset of the Great Depression in 1929, the price of wheat collapsed, making Daniels County farms much less profitable. At the same time, improving farm technology reduced the amount of human labor needed in farm production. As a consequence, and as shown in table 2.2, the number of farms in Daniels County began a steady decline, with a corresponding increase in farm size that has continued to the present. By 2012, there were only about one-third as many farms in the county (338) as there were in 1930. Average farm size increased from 667 acres in 1920 to 2,273 in 2012.

**TABLE 2.2.** Number of Farms and Average Farm Size in Daniels County, Montana, 1920–2012

| Year | Number of Farms | Average Farm Size |
|------|-----------------|-------------------|
| 1920 | 1,020 | 667 |
| 1945 | 675 | 1,196 |
| 1969 | 466 | 1,803 |
| 1987 | 381 | 2,047 |
| 2012 | 338 | 2,273 |

Daniels County is far from urban centers and far from major transportation routes. Thus, the county was largely unsuccessful in attracting the expanding manufacturing sector during the middle decades of the twentieth century. Consequently, as the number of farms declined, there was a corresponding decrease in the number of people living in the county. With few nonfarm employment opportunities, the option of part-time farming was also curtailed. Figure 2.3 presents data showing the steadily declining population of Daniels County. The county population reached a peak in 1930 at 5,553. In 2010, the number of residents in the county was 1,751, only 31.5 percent as many as in 1930.

Driving across Daniels County, it is easy to see why Montana is called "Big Sky Country." With gently rolling hills and a near total lack of trees, it seems as if you can see forever. Grazing cattle and golden wheat waving gently in the late summer breeze contribute to the agrarian feel of the area. Occasionally the road passes a farmhouse, surrounded by farm buildings and equipment. The majority of residents in Daniels County live in the county seat of Scobey. As one approaches Scobey, grain elevators and the town water tower, the tallest structures in town, first become visible. Along Main Street in Scobey only a few businesses are open, including farm supply stores, dollar stores, and convenience stores. Boarded-up and crumbling buildings occupy space where other businesses and shops once stood. On the back streets of Scobey, many of the homes look worn with peeling paint; others are clearly vacant.

The heart of the community is the schools. Enrollment at Daniels County schools has obviously decreased over the decades and now averages about twenty students per grade. As is the case with rural schools everywhere, student opportunities are limited. There are no advanced placement classes, and the range of courses is constrained because there are few teachers. On

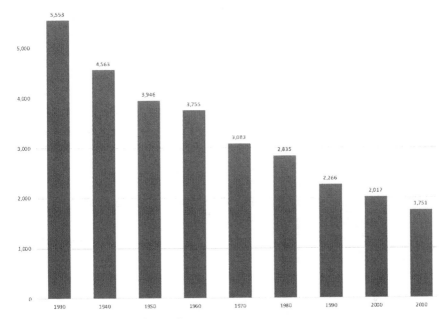

**FIGURE 2.3.** Population of Daniels County, Montana, 1930–2010

average, students in Daniels County score lower than the average Montana student on standardized tests. Because employment opportunities in the county are limited, many young people leave town and never return upon completing high school.

Options to reverse steadily declining population and economic opportunities in Daniels County are limited. Daniels County lacks high-quality amenities that have led to demographic and economic growth in other rural areas. Should these declines continue, eventually it will be very difficult to keep schools open and provide other public services. This is a severe problem because the distance to somewhere else to go to school and shop is daunting. Hoping to halt their slow decline, more than three-fourths of Daniels County voters cast their ballot for Donald Trump in the 2016 presidential election.

## Baca County, Colorado

Baca County is in the extreme southeast corner of Colorado. Baca County borders Kansas to the east and other Colorado counties to the north and west.

The Oklahoma Panhandle and a sliver of New Mexico border Baca County on the south. Traditionally, Baca County was part of the vast southern plains grasslands where herds of bison roamed and the Comanche Indians were the "Lords of the Prairie." Nearly all of Baca County is as flat as a pancake and virtually treeless.

Like the rest of the western Great Plains, cattle ranches were the primary agricultural endeavor following the removal of bison and American Indians. Around the turn of the century, a few farmers moved to the area to home-stead and some of them began growing wheat. As was the case with other parts of the Great Plains, high wheat prices during World War I resulted in the immigration of thousands of homesteaders. Millions of acres of grass-land were plowed under and turned into wheat fields. Following World War I and into the 1920s, wheat prices remained high. Each year it seemed the amount of wheat produced increased, and farmers were doing very well economically. Many farmers were able to replace their sod shanty with a house made of wood. Some purchased a tractor that allowed them to grow even more wheat, and many farmers could even afford a car or pickup truck.

In 1929, life for Baca County residents began to unravel. The 1929 wheat crop was equally good as that of previous years, but unlike in previous years the price collapsed. Years of bumper crops now resulted in a surplus that was made worse by the country descending into the Great Depression. As the Depression worsened, people all over the country were hungry while wheat rotted by the side of the road because there was no market for it. This same pattern occurred with other agricultural commodities. With prices low, the only approach open to farmers to attempt to pay their debts and provide necessities for their family was to plow more grassland and intensify wheat production hoping that the production of more bushels would offset lower prices per bushel. This increased production resulted in continued surplus that kept prices low.

Conditions were then made much worse with the onset of a severe drought beginning in 1930. Year after year, rainfall levels were far below nor-mal. The sun beat mercilessly on the emerging wheat plants, causing them to wither and die. With the prairie grass removed and without crops to hold the soil in place, the incessant prairie wind began to result in increasingly severe dust storms. A region centered on the panhandles of Texas and Oklahoma, the northwest corner of New Mexico, the southeast corner of Colorado (including Baca County) and the southwest corner of Kansas became known as the "Dust Bowl." It was in this region that the fictitious Joad family in *The Grapes of Wrath* (Steinbeck 1939) resided.

Many Dust Bowl storms were so bad that people had to turn on their lights during the middle of the day to see. Respiratory problems emerged, and a number of children and elderly died of what became known as "dust pneumonia." Despite families' best efforts, they were unable to keep fine dust from covering everything inside of their homes. On May 9, 1934, a severe dust storm carried Great Plain soil to East Coast cities such as Washington, DC, and New York. The most severe storm was on a day that became known as Black Sunday (April 14, 1935). This storm was so severe that cars were running off of the road due to a lack of visibility and farmers would get lost trying to walk from their homes to their barns.

By the end of the 1930s decades, the fickle plains rains returned. The onset of World War II brought an end to the Depression, and the price of wheat once again climbed higher. Agriculture in the Dust Bowl region of the Great Plains and Baca County, however, will never again be the same. Some areas most severely damaged by the dust storms lost so much topsoil that agriculture is no longer feasible. Regulations and approaches to farming have also adjusted in an attempt to avoid future dust bowls. Programs now encourage leaving substantial amounts of land in grass and farming using methods that preserve topsoil. Perhaps most significant, the hope and optimism of a century ago are tempered by caution and fear that still remains in the dust bowl region.

Table 2.3 presents data showing the changes that occurred in Baca County. In 1920, there were 1,858 farms there. As was the case in Daniels County, lower prices for wheat, the consequences of the Dust Bowl, and steadily improving technology led to a rapid reduction in the number of farms. By 1969, the number of farms in the county was down to 771, only 41.5 percent as many as in 1920. Since that time, the number of farms in the county has stabilized and there were 737 farms in 2012. The reason for this stability is that Baca County has some benefits lacking in Daniels County. The population is larger, which means more viable communities that can provide off-farm employment, which allows smaller part-time farms to survive.

As was the case in hundreds of other farm dependent counties, a declining number of farms led to reductions in the total population. Figure

**TABLE 2.3.** Number of Farms and Average Farm Size in Baca County, Colorado, 1920–2012

| Year | Number of Farms | Average Farm Size |
|------|-----------------|-------------------|
| 1920 | 1,858 | 558 |
| 1945 | 825 | 1,263 |
| 1969 | 771 | 1,677 |
| 1987 | 612 | 2,132 |
| 2012 | 737 | 2,040 |

2.4 shows population trends in Baca County from 1930 to 2010. Declines were especially dramatic during the Dust Bowl decade of the 1930s before rebounding during the 1940s. Since 1950, population trends in Baca County have been steadily downward. The county's population in 2010 was less than 36 percent of what it had been in 1930 and less than one-half of the 1950 population.

Years of demographic and economic decline are apparent when one drives down Main Street in Springfield, county seat of Baca County. Numerous buildings where businesses and shops once operated are now empty. Many homes are worn and vacant. Hoping to reverse these declines, in the 2016 presidential election more than 81 percent of Baca County voters cast their ballot for Donald Trump.

## The Future of Farm Communities

The initial dominant farm structure in Daniels and Baca Counties and throughout much of the country was a product of the Homestead Act. By early in the twentieth century, millions of relatively small family farms were dispersed across the country—a consequence of policies intended to provide benefits from the farm sector to a large number of individuals and families. Since that time, a variety of factors have combined to drastically change the farm sector from relative equality to extensive concentration. The primary source of change was technological development in which new machines have replaced human labor in the production process.

Through the middle decades of the twentieth century, hundreds of rural counties experienced economic and demographic decline as a consequence of the mechanization of agriculture. What happened in Daniels and Baca

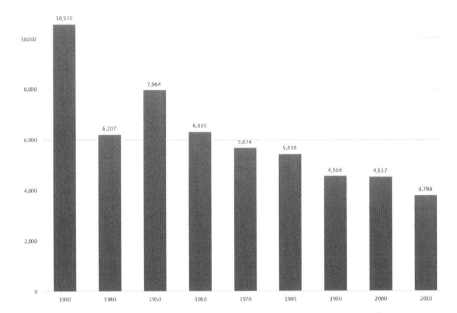

**FIGURE 2.4.** Population of Baca County, Colorado, 1930–2010

Counties was similar to what happened in hundreds of other communities. Many of these places eventually developed alternate sources of employment to offset the declining number of farms. Many rural communities, especially those near urban areas or along major transportation routes, were able to attract manufacturing firms, as was the case in Richland County, Wisconsin (chapter 1). More recently, other communities have been able to use their amenity advantages to develop a tourist industry or to attract persons who have Internet-based jobs and who are thus free to live where they wish. In these counties, the farm sector still exists but typically is now only a small proportion of employment and economic activity in the county. Many small farms exist in these counties where the operator or other family members find part-time employment in the vibrant local economy.

Other farm dependent communities have been unable to attract industry and lack the high-quality amenities to successfully develop an economy based on the service sector. Daniels County, Montana, and Baca County, Colorado, are representative of counties in this category. For decades, the economy and total population of these counties have declined.

Moving forward, agriculture will remain the most basic or fundamental industry in the world. Everyone must eat, and we need the agricultural industry to make that possible. A strong desire exists also to retain a viable farm sector within US borders. The capacity to produce food to support our own population is considered a vital form of national security.

However, the number of jobs in agriculture has been declining for decades, and this decline will continue. Ever improving technology will continue to replace human labor in farm production. Given the uncertainty of immigration in the current political climate, farmers are continually looking for technological solutions to complete necessary farm tasks. Computers and other forms of information technology are contributing to the role of machines continually replacing labor in farming. For example, robots are being used to milk cows on dairy farms. The result of having robots milk cows is that human labor needs decline and the farmer has much more information about the productivity of each individual cow.

There are some things farm communities can do to improve their economic vitality. One of these is "value-added." Value-added is the process of taking resources and rearranging them in ways that make them more valuable. For example, wheat, trees, and cows are converted into loaves of bread, furniture, and hamburgers. The majority of economic value accrues during the value-added process, as a loaf of bread is worth much more than the wheat used in making it. By turning wheat into flour or milk into cheese at the local level, many more dollars can remain in the local community and jobs are created.

The viability of farm communities in the future will depend on their capacity to find other sources of employment and economic activity to replace the ever fewer jobs in agriculture. As will be described in chapter 10, for places such as Daniels County, Montana, and Baca County, Colorado, to achieve economic stability, they need to fully embrace the information and knowledge economy. There are numerous persons who grew up in these counties who would like to return home if there were a way to make a living. By reducing the cost of distance, new technologies open doors to opportunities for making a living that simply didn't exist in the past.

# 3

## The Coal Industry

Coal, like other fossil fuels, was formed from organisms that lived millions of years ago, primarily during the Carboniferous Period (360 to 286 million years ago). Massive swamps with large leafy plants covered most of the earth's surface, and much of the water was thick with algae. As these organisms died, they sank to the bottom of swamps, lakes, and the sea. In time these dead organisms became covered with other organisms and also dirt, rocks, and sand. Eventually, vast amounts of what had once been living organisms were buried hundreds and even thousands of feet below the surface of the earth. Over millions of years, heat and pressure then transformed these organisms into coal, petroleum, or natural gas.

Which fossil fuel was formed from this process was determined by which organisms were involved to begin with, local conditions, time, and the amount of pressure and heat. For example, woody plants most likely became coal, while oil is formed from slimy water plants such as algae. As the total mass of trees exceeds the total mass of algae, there is more coal than oil in the world. There are also differences in the type of coal that was formed.

DOI: 10.7330/9781607329510.c003

Recently formed coal has more moisture and less energy content, while coal under greater pressure for longer periods of time has less moisture and more energy content. Coal types ranging from lower- to higher-energy content are lignite, sub-bituminous, bituminous, and anthracite. In the United States, anthracite coal is only found in northeast Pennsylvania.

Coal is the world's most plentiful fossil fuel. Known coal reserves in the United States exceed the coal reserves in any other country in the world. Energy available from US coal exceeds the amount of energy stored in all of the world's known petroleum reserves. Measured in BTUs, 91 percent of US fossil fuel energy is in coal. For thousands of years, humans have used coal as an energy source for cooking, lighting, and heat. The amount of coal consumed increased dramatically with the onset of the Industrial Revolution. The Industrial Revolution was simply a result of the growing capacity of humans to harness and utilize fossil fuels as an energy source. By using fossil fuel energy, transportation speed and the work capacity of humans all dramatically increased. Following industrialization, coal was used to power the steam engines used in ships, trains, and early factories. Later, when electricity was harnessed, demand for coal skyrocketed further. Coal was then used to generate electrical power that was used to light houses, commercial buildings, and streets and to run appliances in homes and machines for business and industry.

In the United States, large-scale coal mining first emerged in the anthracite region of northeastern Pennsylvania, followed by developments in western Pennsylvania and other parts of Appalachia, where vast coal reserves are found. Much of the coal was then transported by rail from where it was mined to power large eastern and midwestern cities and their industries. From the outset, large companies dominated the coal industry, and the major coal companies employed vast numbers of hired coal miners.

Until recently, nearly all coal in the United States was mined using underground methods. Opening a shaft from the surface into the ground provided access to the coal seam. As miners removed the coal, a growing tunnel emerged that followed the coal seam. Timber was used to provide support to prevent the roof of the growing tunnel from collapsing on the miners. Coal miners would spend the working day deep belowground, where the only available light was what they carried with them. At the mine face, explosives would break coal away from the wall and workers would then shovel the coal into coal cars, which would then transport it to the surface. The coal was then loaded onto trains that carried it to the cities, where it was used. The work was difficult and dangerous.

In early Appalachian coal-mining areas, company towns often emerged near the mine that would provide housing, supplies, and other services for mineworkers and their families. Describing the relationship between the miners and the coal company, Harry Caudill (1963: 174–175) stated:

> He and his family found recreation in the company-owned movie theaters and when he managed to finance a secondhand automobile he bought tires and gasoline for it at the company-owned service station. Company doctors delivered his children, and if the birth occurred in a hospital, the hospital was company-owned. If he was one of the relatively few miners who attended church services, he was likely to do it in a building, which the company owned and thoughtfully provided for the congregation in return for a monthly rent. His school-age children climbed a muddy path up a rock-strewn bank to a company-owned schoolhouse. And, in many instances, when death came from a slate fall or explosion his mortal remains were laid to rest by a company undertaker in a plot of company-owned land.

Because of poor working conditions and low pay, many coal miners were recent immigrants (typically from Eastern or Southern Europe early in the twentieth century) who were desperate for employment. Other miners in Appalachian mines were the already-poor residents of Appalachia (Caudill 1963).

Accidents in coal mines were common. There was constant fear of the roof of the mine collapsing or methane gas in the mines being exposed to a flame and exploding. In 1907, an accident at the Monongah Mine in West Virginia killed 362 miners. Over 3,000 miners were killed in 1907 alone. In the twelve years from 1912 to 1923, 18,243 coal miners were killed in mining accidents, an average of over 1,500 per year (Boal 2009). About half of coal miner deaths were from the collapse of the roof. Other major causes of accidents were coal cars colliding with workers as they traveled back and forth from the surface to where the coal was being mined, and explosions of methane gas and coal dust. Even those who avoided death and injury from accidents often suffered from black lung disease, a condition resulting from breathing coal dust for long periods of time. The coal dust lodges in the miner's lungs and then can neither be destroyed nor removed by the body. Both life expectancy and quality of life were greatly diminished by black lung disease for thousands of miners.

Over the years, better technology and stronger regulations have steadily improved safety in the coal-mining industry (Boal 2009). The danger, however, has not been totally eliminated. In 2010, twenty-nine miners were killed in an explosion at West Virginia's Upper Big Branch coal mine, and in 2007 six miners and three rescue workers were killed at the collapse of the Crandall Canyon coal mine in Emery County, Utah. Mining disasters in other countries with weaker regulations and inadequate technology remain relatively common.

In an effort to advance mine safety and improve pay, there have been near-constant clashes between labor and management and regular efforts by miners to form unions. Management has always strongly resisted union formation, as the changes sought would increase costs and thus reduce profits. In the 1860s and 1870s in the anthracite coalfields of Pennsylvania, sixteen mine officials were assassinated. At the time, it was commonly believed that the culprits were the Molly Maguires, a secret society based in Ireland brought to America by Irish immigrants. A Pinkerton detective named James McParlan claimed to have infiltrated the organization. As a consequence, twenty Irish immigrants were arrested and eventually executed. Recent evidence makes it apparent that rather than being the vicious terrorists as they were portrayed, the Molly Maguires were workers trying desperately to obtain some basic rights, make a living, and be safe in a brutal occupation (Kenny 1998).

Throughout the late eighteenth and early nineteenth centuries, strikes were common and sometimes lethal in the coalfields. In 1897, mine guards killed nineteen unarmed striking miners during the Lattimer strike in the Pennsylvania anthracite coalfields. In Ludlow, Colorado, in 1914, about two-dozen striking union miners were killed by mine guards. The union miners then retaliated and killed sixty-nine mine guards and others. In Herrin, Illinois, three striking union miners were killed. The union miners then retaliated and killed nineteen strikebreaking workers and mine guards. Even when New Deal legislation gave workers the legal right to join unions and bargain collectively, intimidation and coercion were often used to prevent union formation.

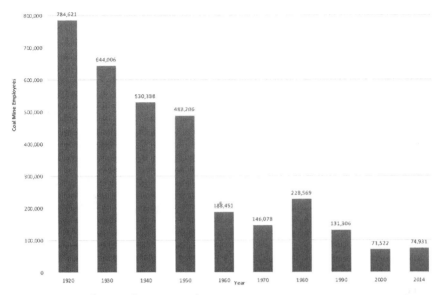

**FIGURE 3.1.** Total US coal miner employment, 1920–2014

The number of coal miners in the United States reached a peak in 1923, with over 800,000 workers. Figure 3.1 shows an extensive and steady decline in the number of coal miners over time, from 784,621 in 1920 to only 74,931 in 2014. Most of this decline can be attributed to improved technology whereby machines replace human labor in the production process. With better technology, miners are more productive, and the amount of coal produced continues to increase despite a much smaller workforce. In underground coal mines of today, massive machines operated by a person with a computer claw huge amounts of coal from the mine face onto conveyer belts that transports the coal to the surface. No longer is it necessary for miners to shovel the coal onto a coal car. Thus, a handful of persons can produce more coal than can hundreds of workers in previous eras. As described below, surface mining is even more productive.

Table 3.1 presents data showing coal production and consumption in the United States from 1950 to 2013. From 1960 until 1990, the amount of coal produced in the United States steadily increased. There was an especially rapid increase during the 1970s following an Organization of Petroleum Exporting Counties (OPEC) embargo. At this time, US petroleum production was

**TABLE 3.1.** Coal Production and Consumption in the United States, 1950–2013 (Quadrillion BTU)

| Year | Production | Consumption |
| --- | --- | --- |
| 1950 | 14.060 | 12.347 |
| 1955 | 12.370 | 11.167 |
| 1960 | 10.817 | 9.838 |
| 1965 | 13.055 | 11.581 |
| 1970 | 14.607 | 12.265 |
| 1975 | 14.989 | 12.663 |
| 1980 | 18.598 | 15.423 |
| 1985 | 19.325 | 17.478 |
| 1990 | 22.488 | 19.173 |
| 1995 | 22.130 | 20.089 |
| 2000 | 22.735 | 22.580 |
| 2005 | 23.185 | 22.797 |
| 2010 | 22.038 | 22.797 |
| 2013 | 20.001 | 18.839 |

*Source*: Energy Information Administration, US Department of Energy Annual Coal Report 2018.

declining, resulting in growing dependence on imports that were largely from OPEC countries. The organization then called an embargo on exports to the United States, reducing energy supplies and dramatically increasing energy prices. The US response was an effort to reduce dependence on foreign energy supplies by increasing production of our most plentiful fossil fuel—coal. A number of new coal-fired power plants were built to reduce dependence on imported petroleum, and new coal mines were opened to produce fuel for these power plants. One of these coal-fired power plants (IPP) is described later in this chapter. Even during periods of increased production, employment levels tend to decline because of the increased capacity of technology.

Not only did coal production increase, but there were also changes in mining methods and location beginning in the 1970s. Table 3.2 shows that in 1950, 75 percent of the coal produced in the United States was from underground mines and 93.6 percent was from mines east of the Mississippi River. Substantial amounts of coal continue to be produced from underground mines and in the eastern states. However, beginning in the 1970s, there have been significant increases in the amount of coal obtained from surface mines

**TABLE 3.2.** Coal Production in the United States by Mining Method and Location, 1950–2014 (Million Short Tons)

| Year | Mining Method | | Location | | Total |
|------|---------------|---------|----------------------|----------------------|--------|
|      | Underground | Surface | East of Mississippi | West of Mississippi | |
| 1950 | 421.0 | 139.4 | 524.4 | 36.0 | 560.4 |
| 1955 | 358.0 | 132.8 | 464.2 | 26.6 | 490.8 |
| 1960 | 292.6 | 141.7 | 413.0 | 21.3 | 434.3 |
| 1965 | 338.0 | 189.0 | 499.5 | 27.5 | 527.0 |
| 1970 | 340.5 | 272.2 | 567.8 | 44.9 | 612.7 |
| 1975 | 293.5 | 361.1 | 543.7 | 110.9 | 654.6 |
| 1980 | 337.5 | 492.2 | 578.7 | 251.0 | 829.7 |
| 1985 | 350.8 | 532.8 | 558.7 | 324.9 | 883.6 |
| 1990 | 424.5 | 604.6 | 630.2 | 398.9 | 1,029.1 |
| 1995 | 396.6 | 636.9 | 544.8 | 488.7 | 1,033.5 |
| 2000 | 373.6 | 700.0 | 507.5 | 566.1 | 1,073.6 |
| 2005 | 368.6 | 762.9 | 493.8 | 637.7 | 1,131.5 |
| 2011 | 345.5 | 748.8 | 455.8 | 638.5 | 1,094.3 |
| 2018 | 275.4 | 480.8 | 310.7 | 445.5 | 756.2 |

Source: Energy information Administration, US Department of Energy Annual Coal Report 2018.

and from mines in the west. With modern technology, surface mining is far cheaper than underground mining, and western coal deposits are more amenable to surface mining. Surface mining involves massive machines that remove soil and other materials covering the coal, extract the coal, and then transport it to power-generating facilities. It is also expected that the land will be rehabilitated after mining is complete.

By 2014, 64.4 percent of the coal produced in the United States was from surface mines and 59.1 percent from western states. Wyoming is now the nation's top coal-producing state, and Campbell County, Wyoming, is the nation's most important coal-producing county. In Campbell County and the Powder River Basin, coal seams from 65 to 100 feet thick are located near the surface and are thus relatively easy and cheap to mine. As a consequence of the mining techniques used in the Powder River Basin, the amount of coal produced per miner per hour is about ten times greater than in Appalachia. Thus, in 2013, Wyoming with 5,837 miners produced more coal than West Virginia, Kentucky, Pennsylvania, Virginia, Alabama, and Illinois combined, with 58,995 miners. It should be pointed out that Wyoming coal is subbituminous while Appalachian coal is bituminous. Because of greater energy content, Appalachian coal is thus more valuable per ton.

Table 3.2 also shows a decline in coal production in recent years. Between 2011 and 2018, the amount of coal produced declined by over 30 percent. As evidence of the decline of the coal industry, Peabody Energy, the world's largest privately owned coal company, declared bankruptcy in April 2016. Peabody joined other coal companies that have experienced a similar fate. A number of factors have combined to place a damper on coal production, discussion of which follows.

## Greenhouse Gas Emissions and Climate Change

Producing energy from coal results in much higher rates of climate-changing greenhouse gas (GHG) emissions than result from alternative energy sources. Growing concern with climate change has resulted in efforts to reduce the amount of coal that is used. Despite attempts by the Trump administration and others to downplay the significance of climate change, policies encouraging cleaner energy are likely to continue and such policies will have harmful effects on the coal industry. For example, proposals have been made to implement a "carbon tax." A carbon tax is a fee on energy emissions to help cover the costs associated with these emissions, including climate change. When implemented, a carbon tax is assessed on the amount of carbon emitted. With this policy, it becomes costlier to utilize energy sources that emit greater amounts of GHGs. The utilization of a carbon tax thus provides incentives for the use of renewable energy by making it costlier to use fossil fuels. In effect, the carbon tax comes close to assessing all of the costs of energy use, including pollution and GHG emissions. As coal is the energy source that emits the greatest amount of GHGs, a carbon tax would be especially harmful to the industry (Metcalf 2009).

## Other Environmental Concerns

Beyond climate change, coal mining has resulted in other troubling environmental problems. Like all mining endeavors, coal mining is environmentally disruptive, and recent changes have resulted in even greater environmental damage. In parts of Appalachia, efforts are being made to make coal production more cost effective by switching from underground to surface-mining techniques. In eastern Kentucky, West Virginia, and southwestern Virginia, "mountaintop removal" techniques have been used in an effort to make surface mining possible. Mountaintop removal involves clearing the forests, stripping the topsoil, and then pushing this dirt and debris into valleys. The coal resources are then accessible to large surface-mining machines (Palmer et al. 2010). The negative environmental implications are extensive. Streams and rivers flowing through the valleys are disrupted and polluted, and wildlife is forced to leave the area. Attempts at rehabilitation have been inadequate. Widespread calls have been made to end this practice (Lindberg et al. 2011).

On several occasions, dams holding coal sludge have broken, causing vast damage downstream. Sludge is a byproduct of ash from coal combustion at coal-fired power plants. On February 26, 1972, the coal slurry impoundment dam in Logan County, West Virginia, broke. The resulting flood along Buffalo Creek killed 125 people. On December 22, 2008, in Kingston, Tennessee, 300 acres were buried under more than a billion gallons of coal sludge after a wall holding back the sludge broke. In addition to the damage to human lives and property, virtually everything in impacted rivers is killed. A similar disaster occurred in Martin County, Kentucky, that is described later in this chapter.

## More Competitive Alternatives

The development of fracking and of horizontal-drilling techniques has reduced the costs of producing oil and natural gas. Often it is now cheaper to use these other fossil fuels with lower GHG emissions instead of coal. Further, renewable energy production is becoming increasingly efficient, making the use of these technologies much more competitive with fossil fuels.

## Coal Communities

Declines in coal-mining production and employment resulting from technological developments have had severe socioeconomic consequences for communities that are economically dependent on the industry. Four coal-dependent communities are discussed in this chapter.

## Martin County, Kentucky

Martin County is located on the eastern edge of Kentucky on the border with West Virginia, deep in the Appalachian Mountains. As with neighboring Appalachian counties, Martin County has extensive coal resources. Significant coal mining began in Martin County early in the twentieth century after the railroad was extended into the region, allowing the coal to be transported to growing eastern and midwestern markets. Since that time, the county has been economically dependent on the coal industry.

Residents of this part of Appalachia were already poor before the coal industry arrived. The relatively poor mountain farmland made it difficult to thrive in agriculture, and isolation made success in other endeavors unlikely. Decades of coal dependence have made poverty an even greater problem. Appalachia is a victim of the "natural resource curse" whereby communities dependent on natural resource extraction have always underperformed economically. This phenomenon has been observed throughout the world and at every level of geography—nations, states and local communities (Van der Ploeg and Venables 2012; Weinstein and Partridge 2014).

Dependence on an export-oriented industry means that high-paying corporate jobs and corporate profits benefit residents living outside of Appalachia. Describing the entire Appalachian region, Harry Caudill (1963: 300) stated: "The nation has siphoned off hundreds of millions of dollars['] worth of its resources while returning little of lasting value. For all practical purposes, the plateau has long constituted a colonial appendage of the industrial East and Middle West, rather than an integral part of the nation generally." Cynthia Duncan (1999) argues that the Appalachian region has experienced a long-term lack of investment—natural resources leave the region, but little of value is returned. Educational investments have been minimal. In fact, the coal industry was happy to limit educational opportunities for their workers because it lessened opportunity for other employment options, thus making workers more dependent on the coal companies. Additionally, protests about working conditions were less likely if miners had little awareness of circumstances elsewhere. In the coal

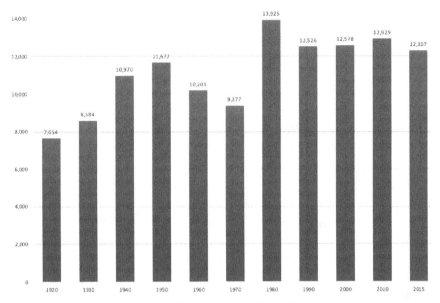

**FIGURE 3.2.** Population trends in Martin County, Kentucky, 1920–2015

mines of that era, not much education was needed to shovel coal all day. Infrastructure investments have primarily been made to make the export of coal and other resources more efficient with little concern for the quality of life of residents.

Places such as Martin County have experienced the brunt of the ups and downs in the coal market. When coal is in high demand and prices are high, miners are able to find work and communities are reasonably prosperous. When demand declines and coal prices diminish, miners are laid off. With few other employment options in the area, unemployment levels skyrocket and community revenues and capacity declines.

Martin County has also had their share of environmental disasters. On October 11, 2000, Massey Energy's coal slurry dam burst. The sludge blackened 100 miles of creekbeds, tainted the town of Inez's water supply, and killed a great deal of aquatic life. A decade later, the impacts were still visible.

Figure 3.2 shows population trends in Martin County. This figure shows that population growth accompanied coal development until after World

War II. Then in the 1950s and 1960s, the coal industry struggled as many industries transitioned from coal to oil as their primary energy source. In Martin County during these two decades, unemployment levels increased, the number of people living in poverty grew, and the total population declined, primarily as a result of young people leaving to seek economic opportunities elsewhere (Vance 2016). During the 1960s, Martin County played a significant role in President Johnson's "War on Poverty." The president visited the county, and widely distributed photos showed him interacting with Martin County residents.

The 1970s brought the OPEC oil embargo and significant growth in coal production. With more jobs in the coal industry, the population of Martin County grew from 9,377 in 1970 to 13,925 in 1980. Since the 1970s, the county has experienced demographic stability and slow economic decline. Even though coal production remained relatively stable, technological developments resulted in the need for fewer workers. The speed of economic decline increased in Martin County as a result of recent efforts to reduce coal consumption, and the impacts in Martin County have been obvious. In 2015, the amount of coal produced in Martin County was only 18 percent as high as it had been in 1995. Even with these drastic declines, the county remains heavily dependent on jobs in the coal mines, as there are few alternative sources of employment. In 2013, 28 percent of the employed labor force in Martin County was directly employed in the coal mines, a higher proportion than in any other Kentucky county.

Indicators of economic distress abound. The most recent Census shows that 40.6 percent of Martin County residents live in poverty and that the median household income is only $28,040. In comparison, the median household income in the United States was $53,657, with 14.8 percent living in poverty. Martin County poverty rates are among the highest in the country. Of great significance are the low levels of educational attainment in Martin County, which translates to a workforce lacking skills to find employment beyond the coal mines. Only 72.7 percent of adults have completed high school, and 7.3 percent have at least a bachelor's degree. In comparison, more than 30 percent of all US adults have a bachelor's degree and about 90 percent have a high school degree. On a positive note for local education, ground was broken in 2017 for the construction of a new high school in Martin County. Like most Appalachian communities,

Martin County is predominately white and about 99 percent of K–12 students are white. However, 65 percent of Martin County students qualify as low income.

The county seat of Martin County is Inez. Like many Appalachian communities, Inez is long and winding with homes and businesses crowded at the bottom of a narrow and meandering valley. The tree-covered hills rise sharply at the edge of town. The scenery is spectacular. While driving through town, there are many vacant and boarded-up buildings. Many of the homes are little more than shacks, often with broken cars and appliances in the front yard.

Like it does elsewhere, poverty in Appalachia closes doors and eliminates opportunities. Opportunities to travel and see what the rest of the world is like are limited, and many people are not aware of options and alternatives available elsewhere. When people attempt to improve their life, their efforts are often like a shaky house of cards. People can work hard to improve their situation, and then the slightest bump in the road brings the whole thing down. For example, the family may work and save to afford an old clunker of a car. With the car, they can obtain work at a location that is farther from home than walking distance. Transportation to work is critical, since public transportation in most rural areas is nonexistent. Then one day, the old car breaks down. Without transportation, the job is lost and the family is back in dire circumstances.

There is little doubt that employment in the coal industry will continue to decline. Even periods of slightly increased production occur would not result in a corresponding increase in employment, because of ever-improving technology. Any changes in the economic fortunes of Martin County are dependent on developing alternative industries. Such development requires a workforce with the requisite knowledge and skills and the infrastructure to support these industries. The achievement of this goal will require extensive and long-term action.

During the 2016 presidential election, Donald Trump promised to save coal-mining jobs by scrapping environmental regulations that provided obstacles to the coal industry and reducing immigration. The consequence was that he received an overwhelming proportion of the vote in coal country. This support is apparent in all of the counties described in this chapter. Nearly 90 percent of Martin County residents cast their vote for Trump.

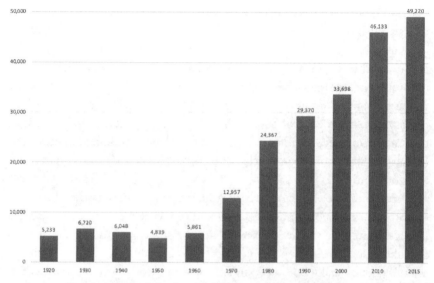

**FIGURE 3.3.** Population trends in Campbell County, Wyoming, 1920–2015

*Campbell County, Wyoming*

Campbell County is located in the northeast portion of Wyoming. Campbell County is a part of the vast treeless Great Plains, with gently rolling hills covered with grass. Herds of pronghorns are common where vast herds of bison once roamed. Historically, Campbell County was economically dependent on ranching and for decades had experienced gradual economic and demographic decline. The 1930 Census counted 6,720 residents in the county; by 1960, this number had fallen to 5,861 (figure 3.3).

Then during the 1970s and following the OPEC embargo, Campbell County and the Powder River Basin became the heart of coal development efforts that were a part of US efforts to become more energy independent. Numerous coal-mining jobs emerged and were quickly followed by construction jobs and employment in coal-fired power plants. In Campbell County and the Powder River Basin, huge seams of coal are found just below the surface. After the soil and rocks covering the coal are removed, very large machines mine the coal. Some coal is transported to nearby power plants, where it is burned; power lines transport the power to cities throughout the West. Other coal is loaded onto trains and transported to more distant power plants.

By 2015, the Campbell County population was 49,220. Coal mining and electricity generation have transformed Campbell County and its primary city, Gillette, from a sleepy ranching community to the nation's most important coal-producing county. As described in the following chapter, early boomtown growth in Gillette led to extensive social problems. Once the community had adjusted to the initial growth, Gillette became a thriving community with good schools and good community services. As coal extraction in Campbell County is based on surface mining, there are few low-skill and low-wage jobs. Many existing jobs in the energy industry require significant skills and pay very well. In fact, in recent years the median household income in Campbell County has been higher than in any other nonmetropolitan county in the West with the exception of Los Alamos County, New Mexico, the home of a major federal research facility. In 2015, the median household income in Campbell County was $78,609.

However, like coal communities everywhere, Campbell County and the Powder River Basin are beginning to feel the effects of the decline of the coal industry. Coal production in Campbell County declined from 404 million tons in 2005 to 328 million tons in 2015. Continued declines will have major implications for the community, as it will be difficult to replace the many well-paying jobs in the coal industry. Because of concern about the future of coal, in the 2016 presidential election, 86.7 percent of Campbell County voters chose Donald Trump.

## Carbon County, Utah

Carbon County earned its name because of extensive coal reserves located in the area. In the late 1800s, significant efforts to mine Carbon County coal began. Typical of coal-mining regions throughout the country at the time, underground mines were used to reach the bituminous coal. Many of the miners were recent immigrants from Eastern and Southern Europe. The consequence was that socially and culturally, Carbon County was very different from the rest of Utah, where the vast majority of residents were Mormon at that time. There is even an Eastern Orthodox Church in Price, county seat of Carbon County.

Like other major coal-mining regions, Carbon County experienced tragedy. In 1900, the Schofield Mine disaster killed 200 miners and in 1924, the

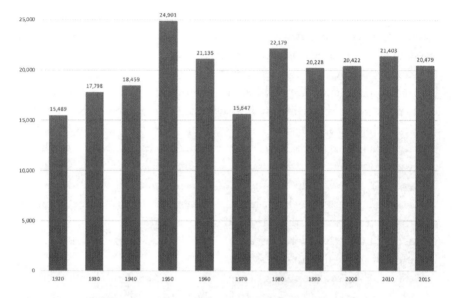

**FIGURE 3.4.** Population trends in Carbon County, Utah, 1920–2015

Castle Gate Mine accident killed 172. A more recent accident in nearby Emery County was mentioned earlier. Like coal-mining regions in other parts of the country, Carbon County had labor unrest and regular conflict between labor unions and management. In a traditionally Republican state, Carbon County generally voted Democrat, and often by substantial majorities as a consequence of the miners belonging to labor unions. The days of labor unions are long gone, however, and in 2016 two-thirds of the votes in the county were cast for Donald Trump.

Figure 3.4 shows demographic trends very similar to those in Martin County, Kentucky. The population in the county increased slowly until 1950, then declined sharply until 1970 as a consequence of reduced demand for coal. Resulting from the coal boom of the 1970s, the population of Carbon County increased from 15,647 in 1970 to 22,179 in 1980. From 1980 until the present, the county has been demographically stable even though coal production has declined.

Economically Carbon County has done much better than coal-mining regions in Appalachia—though not as well as the average American county. In 2015, the median household in Carbon County was $46,366, while 15.7 percent of residents were living in poverty. There are likely several reasons why Carbon County is better off economically than Appalachia. To begin with, the culture and history of the region are very different, and the emphasis on education has been much greater. There is a branch of Utah State University in Price. Also, Carbon County is closer to metropolitan areas and has a more diverse economic sector. It is only sixty miles from Carbon County to the Wasatch Front, where the majority of Utah's residents live. However, continued declines in coal production will have significant economic implications.

This is not to say that Carbon County is flourishing. Many businesses have closed, and the buildings where they once existed are boarded up. Community leaders often talk about the opioid and other drug problems that exist in the community, especially among less-skilled workers who were once employed in the coal mines.

*Millard County, Utah*

Millard County is located in the western part of Utah and borders Nevada. Most of the county is part of the Great Basin Desert. Jagged dry mountains offset vast stretches of sagebrush. Near the city of Delta in Millard County was the infamous Topaz internment camp for Japanese Americans during World War II. The location was chosen because of the remote desert setting. Mormon settlers began moving to the region in the late 1800s, and the economy was based on livestock grazing and irrigated agriculture. As is evident from figure 3.5, the county experienced consistent population declines as agriculture mechanized through the middle decades of the twentieth century. In 1970, the population of Millard County was 6,988, which was a 42 percent decline from the 1930 population.

Despite having no significant coal reserves, Millard County has been greatly impacted by the coal industry and changes therein. As part of US efforts to attain energy independence through increased coal utilization, a determination was made to build a major coal-fired power plant near Delta, Utah, in Millard County. Plans for the project were announced in December 1979, and construction on the Intermountain Power Plant (IPP) began in 1981. Prior to construction in 1980, the population of Delta was about 1,930. The population then exploded to 6,670 in 1984 at the peak of construction (Brown et al. 2005). During the construction boom, "man camps" were built

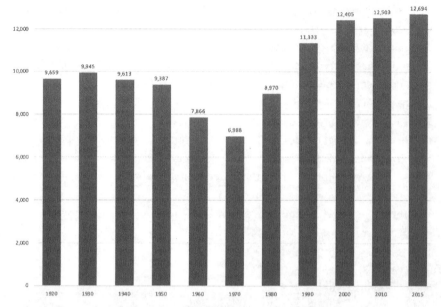

**FIGURE 3.5.** Population trends in Millard County, Utah 1920–2015

to house the primarily young and male workforce. Commercial production of electricity began in 1986. The cost of the facility was $4.5 billion. When operations began, IPP was capable of producing more electricity than any other coal-fired power plant in the nation. Much of the coal utilized by IPP comes from Carbon County and other nearby places in Utah. The majority of the power produced by IPP is sold to Los Angeles County. Thus, an important part of the project was construction of a power line from IPP to Los Angeles.

The implications of IPP for Millard County and the city of Delta were extensive. The most obvious outcome was the extensive economic and demographic growth. During the operation phase, IPP employs more than 400 individuals. Many of them are highly paid engineers, accountants, and other professionals. The consequences are apparent in figure 3.5, which shows Millard County population increased to more than 12,000 by the year 2000. The population of the city of Delta has leveled off at about 3,000. Local businesses have flourished, and the community was able to build new schools, parks, and other facilities.

The problems facing the coal industry are also having major implications for IPP. In 2016, the state of California announced that they would no longer purchase electricity produced by coal after 2020. The fact that the Los Angeles County is IPP's major customer creates significant concern and uncertainty for Delta and Millard County. It is virtually impossible for a small and isolated town in the middle of the desert to replace so many well-paid professional jobs.

Plans are being developed to convert IPP from a coal to a natural gas plant. The cost of this conversion is estimated at about $500 million. Even if IPP survives as a natural gas plant, the economic consequences for the area will be substantial. The number of employees at a natural gas plant is much smaller than the number of employees at a coal plant—perhaps only 10 percent as many. Thus, the adverse economic consequences for the community will still be substantial. As with coal communities everywhere, Donald Trump received a large proportion of the Millard County vote (73.3%). Also, a third-party candidate received more than twice as many votes as Hillary Clinton.

## The Future of Coal Communities

The future of coal is dire because of both environmental concerns and because coal is struggling to compete economically with other energy sources. Even hope of exporting coal to China or other international markets is limited, as these countries are also concerned about the pollution and climate change implications of coal use and are attempting to wean themselves from coal. The coal mining that continues into the future will be ever more mechanized and require fewer workers. A visit to any coal community will reveal a great deal of anger and attempts to find someone to blame for the disruptions that are occurring. In many ways, as we attempt to cope with climate change, we are asking the coal communities to pay much of the cost, while all of us experience the benefits. This is grossly unfair, and as a society we need to help coal communities rebuild their economies. On the positive side, the decline of coal mining means that many of the brutal and dangerous coal-mining jobs that resulted in so many deaths, injuries, and illness over the years are mostly gone forever.

Without question, communities now dependent on the coal industry that desire to be economically viable in the future will need to find a different path for reaching that objective. Instead of spending their time trying to revive a declining industry, communities should instead seek to embrace modern information and communication technology and develop a twenty-first-century economy. Through this path, opportunities exist to develop economic opportunities that have the potential to help coal communities become economically vibrant in the years to come.

# 4

# Fracking, Horizontal Drilling, and Oil and Gas Production

A significant factor leading to the tremendous economic growth occurring in the United States and around the world during the past couple of centuries has been our increased capacity to efficiently utilize fossil fuels. By ever more resourceful uses of oil, coal, and natural gas, our way of life has been completely altered. Fossil fuel energy made transportation faster, industry and commerce more productive, and our residences more comfortable (Albrecht 2014b).

Among fossil fuels, oil has significant advantages. Specifically, as a liquid, it can be widely distributed into homes and also used in transportation. After the discovery of oil at Titusville, Pennsylvania, the demand for oil grew rapidly. Its popularity as a source of light made it possible, in effect, to extend the day. Previously, lamps had used whale oil, an energy source that was relatively rare and expensive. Candles were the other major source of light. The development of automobiles that needed gasoline greatly increased the demand for oil. John D. Rockefeller earned vast fortunes as his Standard Oil Company learned to efficiently refine crude oil into products that could be used and then to distribute it to large numbers of users.

DOI: 10.7330/9781607329510.c004

For several decades in the late nineteenth century, the only known source of commercially viable crude oil was the Pennsylvania fields around Titusville. Great efforts were made to locate additional sources. Eventually oil was discovered in Indiana, then in Texas, Oklahoma, and then other places throughout the world. Early in the twentieth century, "wildcatters" would drill for oil where their hunch led them to believe it could be found. Some even claimed they could smell oil. Unfortunately, most wells were dry, and many life savings were lost. However, those few individuals fortunate enough to strike new energy deposits often became vastly wealthy. In time, growing scientific understanding of geologic formations and improved technology to locate and extract fossil fuels made the quest increasingly efficient (Yergin 1991).

As new domestic resources were discovered and technology continued to improve, US energy production increased. As shown in figure 4.1, US crude oil production grew to more than 9.6 million barrels per day by 1970. Similarly, figure 4.2 reveals steady increases in natural gas production.

Then, despite great financial investment and continually improving science and technology, US crude oil production began to decline. From about 1970 production in several major US oil fields declined as the resource became depleted. The few new fields being discovered were inadequate to offset these declines. Natural gas production leveled off as well. The severity of the decline in US oil production was initially offset by increased yields from Alaska. In the 1960s, what proved to be the largest oil field found in North America to that time was discovered at Prudhoe Bay on the North Slope of Alaska. In 1975 construction began on an 800-mile pipeline from Prudhoe Bay to Valdez, Alaska, the northernmost ice-free port in North America. The pipeline cost an estimated $8 billion to build and opened in 1977. Since that time, over 15 billion barrels of oil have been successfully transported. Prudhoe Bay production has declined in recent years as that resource becomes depleted.

Despite Alaskan production, total US crude oil production continued its rather steep decline. By 2008, US crude oil production was down to 5.0 million barrels per day, barely half as much as in 1970. The implications were immense. Most directly, it became necessary to increase imports from countries with larger available supplies to offset US production shortfalls. Dependence on foreign supplies resulted in the massive transfer of wealth from the United States to major oil-producing countries that resulted in balance of trade concerns. Additionally, the United States spends vast sums on

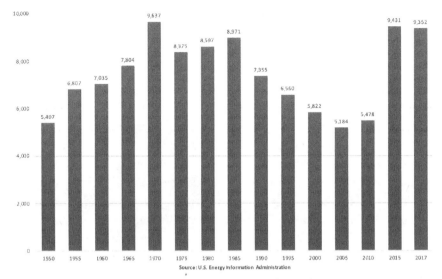

**FIGURE 4.1.** US crude oil production (thousand barrels per day), 1950–2017

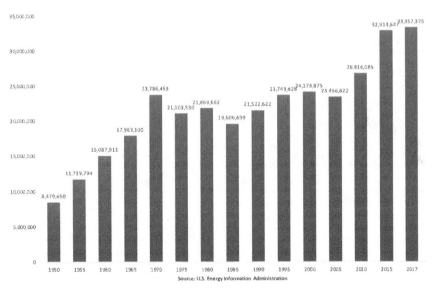

**FIGURE 4.2.** US natural gas production (Mmcf), 1950–2017

military power to assure that our interest in major energy-producing countries is maintained.

Aware of the problems resulting from foreign dependence, US policy has long made a priority of becoming more energy independent, realizing that dependency means vulnerability. Initial emphasis was placed on increased production of coal, our most plentiful domestic fossil fuel, as discussed in the previous chapter (Albrecht 2014b). Emphasis on coal has diminished with growing awareness of GHG emissions and subsequent climate change concerns. There has also been somewhat sporadic support for the development of alternative energy such as renewable and nuclear. Further, steady progress has been made in improving energy efficiency. Modern homes, commercial buildings, industry, and appliances are all much more energy efficient than in the past (Muratori 2014; Oliver 2013). Despite conservation and efficiency efforts, US energy consumption continued to increase as our population and economy grew. Greater consumption meant that dependence on foreign energy supplies continued to expand. By 2005, only 32.9 percent of the petroleum consumed in the United States was produced in the United States.

## Fracking and Horizontal Drilling

Among the most influential technological developments of our time is the emergence of hydraulic fracturing (fracking) and horizontal drilling, new technologies that allow oil and gas to be produced from shale formations (Ferrell and Sanders 2013). Until the past few years, most energy development has been from pools of oil and gas trapped beneath impervious rock formations. For example, in the famous Spindletop, Texas, oil field, the pooled oil was trapped in a salt dome. When drillers reached the oil in the salt dome on January 10, 1901, oil exploded from the well and gushed several hundred feet into the air. Withdrawing oil and gas from these more conventional formations was like sticking a straw (the well) into a glass filled with water (oil) and ice cubes (rocks). Under these circumstances, the oil could rather easily be withdrawn.

Shale formations are fine-grained sedimentary rocks created by the accumulation of deposits at the earth's surface. At times in the geological past, especially if the shale rock was being formed in marshy areas or at the bottom of shallow lakes or seas, these formations were laced with organic materials from dead plants and animals. Over vast geologic time, these shale rocks gradually became covered under newer layers of rock with the effect that they are sometimes buried two or more miles beneath the earth's surface. The resulting pressure and heat that occur deep within the earth then convert the organic materials to fossil fuels such as coal, oil, and natural gas. In shale rock these fossil fuels are trapped within the pores of the rock. Many conventional pools of fossil fuels are actually created by the gradual seepage of oil and natural gas from shale rock through the millennia. The oil and gas that escaped from the shale rock would rise (since it is much lighter than other rocks) until being trapped in pools by higher impervious rock formations.

For example, over the years, energy companies had withdrawn natural gas from wells in northern Texas. These pools of natural gas were formed by gradual seepage from the underlying Barnett Shale (Gold 2014). The depletion of the gas deposits higher in the strata provided motivation to try to find ways to extract natural gas from the underlying Barnett Shale. Efforts by Mitchell Energy, in particular, in the Barnett Shale led to important breakthroughs in the fracking process (Gold 2014; Zuckerman 2013).

For decades, the energy industry was aware that oil and gas were trapped in these tight shale rock formations. The industry was, however, unable to extract sufficient amounts to justify drilling costs. Shale rock was different from conventional pools in that the fossil fuels were trapped in much tighter rock formations. With the oil and gas stuck tightly within the rock formations, a straw stuck into shale rock would be able to extract only very small amounts of oil or gas.

Efforts to break or fracture shale rocks to allow the trapped oil and gas to escape have been attempted for decades. These efforts have included using dynamite and even small nuclear bombs deep inside the earth (Gold 2014). Attempts at hydraulic fracturing (using water at high pressure) have been underway, with limited success, since the 1940s. From the late 1990s, some companies (including Mitchell Energy in the Barnett Shale) began having more success by forcing large amounts of water mixed with sand and chemicals into wells at extremely high pressure. The consequence was that the shale rock would shatter or fracture like glass being struck by a hammer, thus freeing oil and gas molecules and allowing them to flow into the well.

This hydraulic fracturing, or "fracking," process was greatly enhanced by horizontal drilling in which the well is drilled vertically until the oil or gas bearing shale rock formations are reached and then the drill is turned

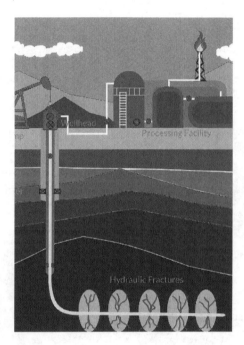

**FIGURE 4.3.** Fracking and horizontal drilling (istockphoto.com)

horizontally to allow a much greater area of contact between the well bore and the energy bearing shale rock (figure 4.3). The fracking and horizontal drilling processes are being continually refined, and drillers are now able to frack wells in stages. That is, one section of the well can be fracked and then later another section. Up to forty stages can be completed until the fracking process has occurred along the full length of the well bore. This process allows the wells to be even more productive. These new technologies have even been used in more traditional wells, where the recoverable oil or gas was largely depleted using traditional extraction methods. For example, by fracking in the Permian Basin of West Texas, production has spiked significantly in wells that previously had declining output.

The implications of fracking and horizontal drilling have been dramatic. Most obvious, domestic energy production has increased substantially. Oil production grew from 5.0 million barrels per day in 2008 to 9.4 million barrels in 2017, an 88 percent increase. Similarly, the production of natural gas increased by 42 percent between 2005 and 2017. As shown in figure 4.4, increased production along with more efficient consumption have led to steadily declining

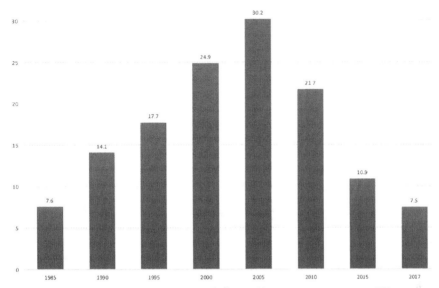

**FIGURE 4.4.** US net energy imports (quadrillion BTU), 1985–2017 (source: US Energy Information Administration)

energy imports. The amount of energy imported into the United States declined by 75 percent between 2005 and 2017. In 2017, energy imports were lower than at any time in the past thirty years. The Energy Information Administration projects that the United States will soon surpass Russia and Saudi Arabia to become the world's largest oil producer and may become energy independent in the next decade or so. Additionally, oil releases 42 percent fewer greenhouse gasses per unit of energy produced than coal. Natural gas is even better, releasing 18 percent fewer GHGs than oil. Thus, increased use of oil and natural gas has allowed less dependence on coal, and this reduction has substantially reduced GHG emissions (Tyner and Taheripour 2014). US GHG emissions reached a peak in 2007 and were 11 percent lower by 2016. US GHG emissions in 2016 were the lowest since 1993. China has now surpassed the United States as the world's largest producer of GHGs.

## Fracking Concerns

Despite significant and obvious benefits resulting from fracking, several concerns have been raised. These issues and concerns are most pertinent at the local community level (Weinstein and Partridge 2014). In effect, most Americans, regardless of where they live and how they feel about fracking, benefit to some degree from this process. Fracking has resulted in lower energy prices, reduced GHG emissions, and less foreign energy dependence. At the same time, while benefits accrue to some local community residents (often substantial), local residents also bear a much higher share of the costs. Because of these concerns, a number of communities and even the state of New York have placed moratoriums on fracking. Generally, concerns with fracking can be placed into two major categories: environmental and community (the latter of which includes economic; Ferrell and Sanders 2013).

*Environmental Concerns*

The residents of communities living near major energy developments are going to experience varying degrees of environmental disruption. Some may be mere nuisances; others could be significant health hazards. These environmental issues are listed below.

CONTAMINATION OF GROUNDWATER SUPPLIES. About 99.5 percent of the fluid forced into wells to fracture shale rocks is water. The fluid also consists of some sand that is intended to lodge into pores of the fracked rock to allow more oil or gas to escape. Some chemicals are also used. Which chemicals are used and in what proportion are unknown and considered proprietary. Of course, uncertainty causes discomfort. Wells are often drilled through groundwater supplies before reaching the energy-laced shale rock. Fears have been expressed that fracking fluids or oil and gas being drawn from the well will escape and contaminate groundwater supplies either by accident, whereby the well bore breaks, or from seepage upward from the fractured shale rock to the groundwater supply. To guard against this eventuality, laws require that well bores be encased in cement to prevent leakage until the well bore is below groundwater levels. Likewise, there is concern about disposal of fracking fluids after their use, again based on uncertainty regarding fracking fluid content.

DEPLETION OF SCARCE WATER SUPPLIES. The fracking process uses vast amounts of water and this places stress on other water users, especially in the water scarce west.

REDUCED AIR QUALITY. There are concerns that air quality will be reduced by drilling activities and dust rising from the tremendous increase in truck traffic. Rural gravel roads previously used mainly by a few farmers now have up to 800 trucks traverse them in a single day (Weinstein and Partridge 2014). Both health problems and reduced visibility are potential outcomes.

NOISE POLLUTION. Energy development means large machines running around the clock, as well as the significant increase in truck traffic mentioned earlier. The constant noise can be a burden for those living near developments.

WILDLIFE DISRUPTION. Drilling activity and new roads being built to service widely scattered wells mean that wildlife experience disruptions and fragmented habitat. This problem is all the more significant in areas where vulnerable populations, such as sage grouse, live.

POTENTIAL EARTHQUAKES. Recent evidence indicates that fracturing rocks deep within the earth causes numerous microearthquakes in some sensitive areas. The extent to which fracking may cause more severe earthquakes is an issue of obvious concern (Ellsworth 2013).

REDUCED EMPHASIS ON RENEWABLE ENERGY. The tremendous increase in domestic energy production resulting from fracking may lead to reduced interest in and funding for renewable energy development. Rapid increases in production resulting from fracking and horizontal drilling led to lower energy prices that reduced the interest of many people in renewable energy. Some critics of reliance on fracking argue that reduced emphasis on renewable energy would be a mistake because, like all fossil fuels, oil and gas in shale rock are a finite resource. Projected dates for depletion of our fossil fuel reserves have been moved back because of recent technological developments but still lurk sometime in the future. Further, even though GHG emissions have been reduced with the advent of fracking, the accumulation of GHGs in the atmosphere continues to increase. Greenhouse gas emissions are a global issue, and whether emitted in the United States, China, or elsewhere the potential remains for catastrophic outcomes. Consequently, improvements in renewable energy production must be continued.

*Community Impacts*

From the outset, wherever major fossil fuel developments occurred, community impacts have been substantial. The first major oil boom in this country followed the discovery of oil in Titusville, Pennsylvania, in 1859 by Edwin Drake. Following Drake's discovery, the population exploded, new jobs were created, and fortunes were made and lost. A small and quiet community became rampant with activity and not all of it to the liking of longtime residents. Russell Gold (2014) described what happened to Burkburnett, Texas, when oil was discovered there in 1919. He noted that jobs were created, business sales expanded, restaurants had sufficient clientele to stay open around the clock, and schools benefited from increased revenue. At the same time, the streets were turned to a fetid mess, dance halls were closed for "immoral" activities, and there was even a drug bust. Life in what was once a quiet and peaceful rural community was drastically altered.

In Oklahoma, oil was discovered under land given to the Osage Indians in what is now Osage County. Soon the Osage were among the wealthiest people in the world, which led to attempts by non-Osage to get some of that wealth during the 1920s and included the murder of numerous Osage and the eventual establishment of the FBI (Grann 2017).

More recently, as a part of efforts to increase coal production to offset petroleum production declines in the 1970s, Gillette (Campbell County), Wyoming, was transformed from a sleepy ranching community to the nation's most important coal-producing area. During the initial development when the population exploded, Gillette experienced a variety of social disruptions that together became known as the "Gillette Syndrome." Symptoms of the Gillette Syndrome include high crime rates, high rates of alcohol and drug abuse, degraded mental health, and weakened social and community bonds (Brown et al. 2005; Kohrs 1974; Smith et al. 2001). The outcomes have been similar in other energy boomtowns. In each case, the community reaps considerable benefits but also pays significant costs.

Three overriding factors are relevant in discussions of community impacts of energy development. Each of these three will be apparent in discussions of the specific examples that follow. First, costs and benefits are not distributed equally among community residents. Some residents receive substantial economic benefits; others receive few direct economic benefits and instead experience substantial costs.

Second, it should also be recognized that the extent of community impacts varies greatly by community size. Energy development can occur wherever resources are found. Some of these sites may be under or near major metropolitan areas. For example, the Barnett Shale underlies the western half of the Dallas–Ft. Worth metropolitan area. A major city has the capacity to meet additional demands for housing, school classrooms, and hospital beds as a matter of course. Additionally, there are wide-ranging entertainment options in cities available for energy workers. On the other hand, rapid growth resulting from energy development often occurs far from any urban area. Thus, development of the Bakken Shale has centered in rural western North Dakota where the few and scattered communities are all quite small. Further, there are no cities nearby where workers could live and commute from. Small towns lack the necessary housing, other infrastructure, and entertainment options and generally lack the capacity for quick development to meet these needs.

Third, when an energy boom occurs, a corresponding bust eventually follows (Christopherson and Rightor 2014). When the resource on which the boom was based is depleted, the jobs and economic activities vanish. Additionally, wide price swings can result in the expansion and contraction of development efforts. The environmental damage, however, remains. Numerous studies have found that counties, states, and even nations that are heavily dependent on a resource-based economy tend to have long-term economic struggles—the "resource curse." The exception appears to be larger cities that contain industry headquarters, such as Houston, Texas (Weinstein and Partridge 2014). Thus, even while coping with a boom, communities need to be planning for the eventual bust.

MINERAL LEASES AND ROYALTIES. Prior to development, oil and gas companies send representatives to the area to present mineral right owners with a contract that when signed gives the industry the legal right to extract resources from beneath the surface. Generally, but not always, the owner of the surface land also owns the minerals beneath the surface. Sometimes, however, the owner of the surface land and the owner of the minerals are different. Oil and gas companies typically pay a per-acre fee to lease mineral rights in addition to royalty payments for any producing wells (Fitzgerald 2014). For some landowners, specifically some farmers and ranchers with large landholdings, this income could be significant. Unfortunately, some may live near the energy development, but not own the mineral rights or not have minerals underneath their land. These persons thus have to cope with the costs of development, but do not economically benefit from lease payments or royalties.

Further, the extents to which people benefit from mineral leases may vary by socioeconomic status, with more disadvantaged persons tending to sign less advantageous mineral lease contracts. Disadvantaged status included persons with lower levels of educational attainment and lower incomes. Especially significant, Hispanics with less English-language proficiency often sign less advantageous leases.

JOBS AND WAGES. Most rural areas deal with the persistent problem of too few jobs and inadequate pay for existing jobs. One of the major attractions of energy development for local communities is the potential for more and better jobs. Unfortunately, research indicates that the number of jobs in the energy industry obtained by residents of local communities is not as extensive as indicated by media reports. Most locals who do get energy jobs tend to get jobs that are lower skilled and thus lower wage (Weinstein and Partridge 2014). Most fracking jobs require specialized skills, and companies tend to import workers with the requisite skills. Typically, workers with the specific skills needed at a fracking worksite work at one site until the job is completed and then move to the next job site.

The issue of jobs for local communities is made more complex because the size of the labor force during the construction phase (when wells are being drilled and fracked) is far greater than during the operation phase (when the well is producing oil or gas). During the operation phase, a relatively small number of workers who are well educated and highly trained can keep the wells running and the process moving forward. Again, because of the skills required, these operation phase workers are likely to be imported. It should be noted that in a major energy development area, such as the Bakken formation in North Dakota, construction and operation are occurring simultaneously and may continue to do so for some time. Wells are being drilled and fracked and then brought into operation while new wells are being drilled and fracked.

The high demand for labor does tend to result in higher wages. Employers from fast-food restaurants to grocery stores to farms and ranches are forced to pay higher wages in order to attract workers. Of concern is that some of these employers (such as farmers and ranchers) have to pay higher wages but do not necessarily receive higher prices for their products; thus, business profitability is reduced. Furthermore, some residents of energy boomtowns are unable to benefit from higher wages and other economic opportunities that emerge in their community. For example, retired people living on a fixed income are likely to experience higher housing and other costs, more noise and congestion, and perhaps even a greater fear of crime while receiving few economic benefits.

GROWTH OUTSTRIPPING AVAILABLE INFRASTRUCTURE. Importing large numbers of workers often quickly overwhelms local infrastructure, especially in small towns. As new residents move in, housing becomes scarce and thus often expensive (Fernando et al. 2018). Water and sewer systems are overwhelmed, roads are overcrowded, and schools and hospitals lack space for their expanding clientele. The option for communities to plan and prepare in advance for the influx of new workers is difficult because the labor force during the construction phase often greatly exceeds the number of workers that will be needed during the operation phase.

A common approach by industry and communities is to develop "man camps" for workers during the construction phase. These man camps are dormitory-like establishments that typically provide workers with a small room that includes a bed, a desk, and a TV. Cafeteria-type meals are provided, and bathroom and shower facilities are shared. Since a vast majority of workers are male, families and children are often excluded. In time, revenues generated by the development are likely to bring community infrastructure in line with community size.

BOOMTOWN EFFECTS. Especially during the construction phase, the imported workforce tend to be young, mostly male, and often single. Since construction phase jobs are temporary and housing and other infrastructure are inadequate, married workers often do not bring their families. The consequences of having large numbers of young, well-paid, single men who live in man camps in rural communities with limited opportunities for entertainment during nonwork hours are predictable. The problems currently being experienced in rural North Dakota are similar to those experienced by Titusville, Pennsylvania, Burkburnett, Texas, and Gillette, Wyoming during previous eras. Rural communities that were once peaceful and quiet now become racked with a variety of social problems ranging from drug use and prostitution to conflict between new and longtime residents. In some ways, modern energy boomtowns resemble the nineteenth-century wild-west mining communities.

## Williston, North Dakota

Williston is the regional service center for a large portion of northwest North Dakota and eastern Montana. The city of Williston is located on the

Missouri River near its confluence with the Yellowstone River. Williston is in Williams County and just across the river from McKenzie County. For decades, the primary industry in the region was farming and ranching. As agriculture mechanized during the middle decades of the twentieth century, the population in the region slowly eroded. In McKenzie County, the population in 1930 was 9,709; eighty years later, in 2010, the population was 6,360, a decline of 34 percent (figure 4.5). As the regional center, Williston was better able to retain a more stable population. In 1980, the population of Williams County was 22,237. Thirty years later in 2010, the number of residents was virtually unchanged at 22,398 (figure 4.6).

Williston overlies the Bakken Shale, a formation that is likely to produce more oil than Prudhoe Bay and become the highest producing formation in US history. Since the emergence of fracking, the speed and magnitude of development in the Williston area have been astounding. In 2005, North Dakota crude oil production was 35.7 million barrels; in 2015 production was more than 10 times greater, at 430 million barreols (figure 4.7). As a consequence of reduced prices, there was a reduction in production by 2017.

With such dramatic development, the population of Williams County increased by 58 percent to 35,294 in just five years from 2010 to 2015 (figure 4.6). In nearby McKenzie County, after years of slow population declines, the number of residents more than doubled in just five years (figure 4.5). Although substantial, these numbers fail to capture the full magnitude of the transition, as many workers are transient and are not counted by the Census Bureau during their short tenure in the community. Amanda Weinstein and Mark Partridge (2014) report that employment in Williams County increased from less than 13,000 in 2005 to more than 28,000 in 2011. They also report that per-capita income increased by 166 percent between 2005 and 2011 and was over $81,000 in 2011.

Such rapid growth has resulted in the emergence of the boomtown problems of overburdened infrastructure and in an increase in crime, prostitution, and other social problems. Intoxication and fights are common in downtown Williston. Rapid growth surpassed the community's ability to provide housing. Consequently, in 2013 the costs of rental housing were the highest in the nation. To attract workers, Walmart is forced to pay twenty dollars per hour. Big trucks roll through the streets twenty-four hours per day, disturbing the peaceful serenity that once existed in this outpost in the prairie. Hoping for

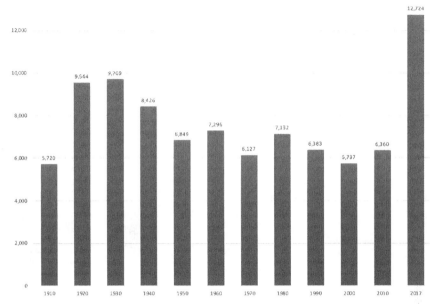

**FIGURE 4.5.** Population trends in McKenzie County, North Dakota, 1910–2017

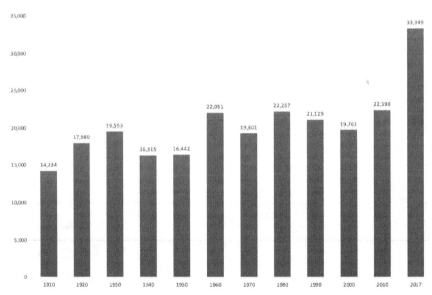

**FIGURE 4.6.** Population trends in Williams County, North Dakota, 1910–2017

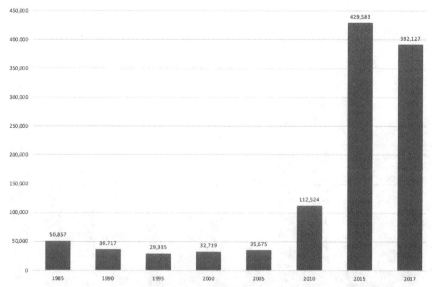

**FIGURE 4.7.** North Dakota field production of crude oil (thousands of barrels), 1985–2017 (source: US Energy Information Administration)

policies that will continue to support resource development, 78.6 percent of Williams County residents voted for Donald Trump in the 2016 presidential election.

## The Future of Energy Development Communities

The benefits to the nation from fracking and horizontal drilling are extensive, and there is no question these technologies are here to stay. The emergence of fracking and horizontal drilling has substantially altered the energy future for the United States. After decades of declining production and increased dependence on foreign imports, the United States is on the verge of becoming the world's number one producer of crude oil and may soon become energy independent. Increased oil and natural gas production have also meant less dependence on coal, which in turn has resulted in declining GHG emissions.

Numerous communities throughout the country that overlie shale formations have experienced very rapid economic and demographic growth as a result of energy development. Energy development brings significant economic opportunities to impacted communities and at the same time has the potential to bring considerable environmental and community costs. Long experience has taught us that dependence on energy development as a community development strategy has significant limitations. Communities ride the roller coaster of rising and then declining prices that make stability most difficult to achieve. Further, resources are finite and when the energy resource is depleted the economy will decline. The oil and gas industry will become more mechanized in the years to come, and consequently employment opportunities will decline.

The energy industry can be an important part of a community developing a healthy diversified economy. For communities dependent on oil and gas development to become economically viable and stable, it is essential that they take full advantage of emerging opportunities that are a part of a twenty-first-century information and knowledge economy. This flexibility will allow the development of stable jobs that will help these communities withstand the ups and downs of the energy development.

# 5

# Northwest Forests and the Logging Industry

Along the Pacific Coast, from Alaska and British Columbia through Washington, Oregon and into Northern California, are vast expanses of truly incredible temperate forests. Made possible by extensive rainfall, early settlers found massive trees from the crest of the Cascade Mountains to the coast. Some of these trees were hundreds of years old, approaching 300 feet high and growing in forests so dense that travel was made difficult by the tangle of underbrush and fallen trees. While the Redwood Forests of Northern California were homes to the tallest living organisms on the planet, the northwest forests in their entirety were among the most spectacular and productive on earth.

While the economic potential of these forests was apparent, the trees were also an obstacle to transportation and agriculture, and great efforts were made, with near universal support, to cut the trees and put them to some productive use. The forest industry began rather slowly. Most of the trees that were harvested were only used locally because of transportation difficulties. Further, in the expansive coastal forests, available technology made cutting the large

DOI: 10.7330/9781607329510.c005

trees extremely challenging. Workers would labor for several days with axes and saws to fell a great tree, only to have the tree land upon and become entangled with other large surrounding trees. Working with these massive trees was also extremely dangerous, and injuries and even death were relatively common (Darby 1967; Dietrich 1992).

Through the latter decades of the nineteenth century and early decades of the twentieth century, continually improving technology led to a rapidly growing timber industry. Mills were built by the side of rivers, where the current could be used to generate power to operate equipment to cut the trees into boards that could be used for building. Later, steam power made this equipment even more efficient. A major breakthrough involved employing steam power to operate "steam donkeys." These machines allowed attaching chains to fallen trees that could then be dragged for a mile or more to a mill or to the edge of the river, where they could be floated to a mill. Prior to the invention of the steam donkey, teams of oxen would be employed to drag trees from where they were cut to where they could be used.

A later improvement to this system was the "high-lead" whereby high-suspended cables allowed one end of the tree to be lifted into the air and then pulled to where the tree was needed with the other end dragging on the ground. Also, of significance, the invention and continual improvement of the gasoline-powered chainsaw allowed forest workers to greatly increase the number of trees that could be cut compared to using the ax and saw. The expansion of the railroad was critical to the growth of the timber industry, allowing lumber to be transported to meet demands of expanding urban markets in other parts of the country and throughout the world. As technology improved, the northwest timber industry grew steadily, with only occasional periods of stagnation or decline during times of economic recession when the construction industry stalled. Technological developments resulted in steady progress toward increased domination of the timber industry by larger companies and corporations, and a growing proportion of workers were employees of these companies. The timber industry reached its zenith in 1988, when nearly 15.7 billion board feet were harvested in the states of Washington and Oregon combined.

Timber was initially harvested in areas where trees were most accessible—near cities, highways, or rivers and where mountains could be avoided. As these areas were harvested, the timber industry gradually expanded into more remote and difficult areas. In time, the timber industry became a major economic driver, and many communities throughout the region became heavily dependent on jobs in all segments of the timber industry (LeMonds 2001). Logging provided not only relatively well-paying jobs, but also a definition of place and was deeply embedded in community culture. Logging was an occupation that "real men" worked. Lumberjacks would enter the forests carrying their chainsaws for cutting down massive trees. Others had jobs climbing tall trees or cutting them into boards that could be used to build homes or businesses. The work was physically demanding and dangerous, but many timber workers felt they were doing something important and felt pride in their work (Sherman 2005, 2006, 2009). An added benefit was that many timber workers perceived working outdoors as a positive feature, even though they were often working in the rain and cold (Dietrich 1992; LeMonds 2001).

With a seemingly endless supply of trees, there was little concern expressed for the ecological impacts of the logging industry. During early years, the timber industry had tremendous negative environmental implications in the Northwest and in other parts of the country. It was largely an opportunistic industry because only the most valuable trees were harvested and the cut-and-run patterns left millions of acres drastically altered (Kelly and Bliss 2009). As the steam donkeys would drag the large trees, they would tear up the soil and destroy smaller trees. A huge volume of biomass waste was left, increasing the potential for destructive forest fires as the biomass dried. With the protective plant cover removed and the soil torn by the steam donkeys, rainfall would result in extensive amounts of silt washing into rivers and streams, which played havoc on fish and other aquatic life. Little effort was made to replant, and the eroded soil was often permanently damaged, inhibiting the capacity of the environment to grow trees in the future.

Northwest timberlands are managed by three major categories of owners that have very different objectives. Proportionally, the largest owner of timberland in the Pacific Northwest is the federal government. Extensive federal ownership of forestland occurred because homesteaders in the settlement era recognized that they would be unable to make a sustainable living on 160 acres of forestland. Thus, the land remained unclaimed and in federal ownership. For example, in Oregon 57 percent of forestland is federally owned. Nearly all federal timberland in the Northwest is managed by three agencies—the

US Forest Service, the Bureau of Land Management (BLM), and the National Park Service. Each of these agencies has different goals with respect to trees and the land. From the time of their formation, the US Forest Service and BLM emphasized that resources (including trees) should be used but only sustainably. Thus, from the beginning, timber was harvested on land managed by these two agencies. Since trees are a renewable resource, it was felt that they could be harvested at a rate at which the trees cut down would be replaced by growing trees in a manner to assure a continual supply of timber.

While these agencies were responsible for all resources within their lands, there is no question that management emphasis was given to the commercially valuable trees. There was little concern for the myriad other species that inhabited the forest—with the possible exception of large mammals that people like to hunt. The importance of federal agencies in the northwest timber industry was significant, and in 1988 when the timber harvest reached its peak, 41.1 percent of the total board feet in Oregon and Washington were from US Forest Service and BLM lands.

The emphasis of the third federal agency, the National Park Service, is very different from that of the US Forest Service and BLM. The Park Service's Organic Act states that the purpose of National Parks is to "conserve the scenery and the natural and historic objects and the wild life therein and to provide for the enjoyment of same in such manner and by such means as will leave them unimpaired for the enjoyment of future generations." With emphasis on preservation and retention of nature, Park Service policy has forbidden timber harvest. While much Park Service land in the Northwest is extremely scenic high alpine areas of rock and ice, parts of National Parks such as Mt. Rainier, Olympic, and North Cascades have also preserved large segments of old growth forest with vast numbers of massive trees.

A second major category of northwest timberland is privately owned land. In 1988, 50.7 percent of the board feet harvested in Washington and Oregon were from private lands. Large timber companies own a predominant share of private timberlands, thus solidifying the role of large corporations in the timber industry. Large amounts of private timberlands were once owned by the railroads. Railroads were given vast amounts of land in a checkerboard pattern to encourage railroad construction. Much of this land was later sold to private timber companies. For example, in 1900 Weyerhaeuser bought 900,000 acres of timberland from the railroads for six dollars per acre. By 1903,

Weyerhaeuser owned 1.3 million acres of forestland in the Pacific Northwest (LeMonds 2001). In recent decades, these companies generally have managed their land as a large tree farm. As trees are harvested, new species of trees chosen for their economic value are replanted. The primary goal of private timber companies is to make a profit, and thus there is less emphasis on preservation or biodiversity.

A significant amount of timber is on land owned by small private landholders. With small landholders, commercially valuable trees are growing on land managed primarily as farmland or simply part of the family homestead. Generally timber management is not a major priority, but the benefit of occasionally having commercially valuable trees available to harvest is a bonus. In most cases, small landholders lack the technology or skills to harvest the trees growing on their land and necessarily employ timber companies for this purpose.

The third entity owning significant proportions of northwest timberland is other public entities including state, county, and city governments and Indian tribal land. In 1988, the remaining 8.2 percent of timber board feet harvested in Washington and Oregon came from these lands. Management objectives vary widely on these lands.

As the years passed and the timber industry expanded, it became apparent that old-growth forests were being depleted. Recognition of this unsustainable harvest, however, did not cause much alarm. It was argued by a variety of that after the old growth was harvested, a new crop of trees would soon be growing to replace those that had been cut. In fact, the view at the time of the general public, the US Forest Service, and even university forestry departments was that removal of massive old-growth trees was a good thing. These trees were hundreds of years old, and many of them were decaying and dying. It was felt that as the old growth forest was removed, younger, faster-growing, and more productive trees could replace these massive, ancient trees. It was also felt that old-growth forests were biological deserts and that wildlife would thrive better in younger and more vibrant forests.

## Changes in the Forest

Beginning in the 1980s, circumstances changed dramatically in northwest forests. Two factors are paramount to these changes. First, it became apparent that the forests were being harvested unsustainably and that trees were being cut at a much faster rate than they could grow back. While initially not considered a problem, it soon became apparent that the much smaller trees in second- and third-growth forests were simply unable to replace the total board feet of massive old-growth trees that had taken centuries to grow. It became obvious that even Forest Service land, which from the beginning had supposedly been managed to provide a continuous supply of timber, was being harvested unsustainably. David Clary's (1986) history of the Forest Service argues that the Forest Service was subverted by the timber industry from the beginning and that trees were often being removed four times faster than they could grow back. Generations of Forest Service employees had been evaluated and promoted based on the amount of timber that was harvested in their jurisdiction.

By 1990 it was estimated that 90 percent of the original old-growth forest in the Northwest had been removed. For the timber industry, the number of board feet that could be harvested was in decline, resulting from the overharvesting that had occurred in the past. Additionally, technological developments were resulting in the need for fewer timber workers. A smaller workforce with better technology could harvest more timber than a much larger workforce could harvest previously. This reduced employment was already beginning to impact timber towns.

The second factor leading to change in northwest forests was the emergence and growth of "ecological" forestry, a way of looking at the forest based on expanding scientific knowledge. Ecological forestry places emphasis on the overall health of the forest, biodiversity, and the thousands of species comprising the forest community, rather than solely on a few species of commercially valuable trees (Fortmann and Fairfax 1991; Hays 2007, 2009).

As scientists looked closer at old-growth forests, they found that they were far from biological deserts but rather home to a wide range of life. Dead and dying trees, even the rotting logs lying on the forest floor, were critical for the life of many species. Many plants, animals, and microbial organisms were equipped to live in the unique environment provided by old-growth forests and would struggle in any other situation (Lindenmayer and Franklin 2002). Researchers found the old-growth forest provided numerous additional ecological benefits, such as contributing to clean air and water. Further, replacing natural and especially old-growth forests with plantation forests or tree farms has been found to significantly reduce biodiversity (Brockerhoff et al. 2008). Additionally, researchers found that salmon and other aquatic animals were healthier and more abundant in streams flowing through old-growth forests relative to streams flowing through areas that had been logged (Helfield and Naiman 2001). As ecological forestry grew in importance, long-standing assumptions about the forest and how to calculate its value began to change and many argued that simply assigning dollar signs to large trees was much too narrow of a measure.

As concern and respect for old-growth forests grew, battle lines began to form. The timber industry and logging towns were on one side and desired to continue to harvest trees and reap employment and other economic benefits. The industry recognized that trees were being harvested unsustainably, and it would be necessary to slow down their rate of harvest. Industry leaders felt, however, that since trees are a renewable resource they could and should continue to provide wood for homes and other buildings critical to our lifestyle and economy into the foreseeable future. Timber town residents, whose jobs and the economic vitality of their community were based on logging, generally supported continued tree harvest. Timber workers had experienced some job compression for years, as continually improving technology resulted in ever fewer jobs; they were concerned about the greater rate of job loss that would result from reduced timber harvests.

On the other side were environmentalists and others who examined the scientific research and then placed high priority on preserving the few remaining segments of old-growth forests for their biodiversity and the other ecological benefits. This camp argued, further, that all forms of life have a right to exist and that their worth should not be based on their economic value to humans.

As the controversy began to unfold, the northern spotted owl made its initial appearance onto American consciousness (figure 5.1). Northern spotted owls (Strix occidentalis caurina) live in old-growth forests in the Pacific Northwest. They survive primarily by hunting small rodents, almost exclusively at night. Given that these owls are very uncommon, only move around at night, and live in dense old-growth forests, they are rarely seen. In fact, many people who have spent a lifetime in northwest forests have never seen a spotted owl. Beginning in the 1970s, researchers found that spotted owls are one of the species that thrive in old-growth forests and don't do well in other

**FIGURE 5.1.** Northern spotted owl (istockphoto.com)

environments. As old-growth forests were diminished, owl numbers were declining and it became apparent that a key factor to spotted owl survival was retention of old-growth forests.

It quickly became obvious to environmentalists that the spotted owl, used in conjunction with the Endangered Species Act of 1973, provided a powerful tool to wield in their efforts to protect old-growth forests. The question of how much old-growth forest was needed for spotted owl survival was a topic of intense research, speculation, and disagreement. The timber industry was quick to point out that significant amounts of old-growth forest were preserved in the National Parks. The ensuing debate was never really about owls; rather, the owl was simply a surrogate or instrument in the battle between political rivals over the question of development versus conservation. The owl's significance became apparent on June 26, 1990, when the US

Fish and Wildlife Service declared the northern spotted owl as "threatened" on the Endangered Species List. The implications were profound, as later court orders required protection of large amounts of old-growth forest for spotted owl habitat, much more than existed in the National Parks.

The data in figure 5.2 show extensive and rapid declines in timber harvests; especially on federal land following regulations intended to protect the spotted owl. In 1988, more than 6.4 billion board feet of timber were harvested on federal land in Washington and Oregon. The number of board feet harvested had declined by 44.8 percent just two years later, in 1990. By 2001, timber harvest on federal land in Washington and Oregon had been reduced to only 252 million board feet, or a 96 percent reduction from 1988. In 1988, 41.1 percent of northwest timber harvest came from federal land; by 1990 this proportion had been reduced to 29.4 percent and by 2001 was down to only 3.5 percent. Since about 1990, nearly every proposal for a timber harvest on federal land has been challenged on ecological grounds, and litigation is commonplace. Timber harvests on private and other lands have been much more consistent but have been unable to take up the slack resulting from federal reductions. Figure 5.2 shows that while being relatively steady throughout the years of the spotted owl controversy, private land harvests took a major dive in 2008 and 2009 as a result of the Great Recession. Timber harvest then began to bounce back as economic conditions improved. Overall, however, northwest timber harvests have been substantially reduced.

Implications of reduced timber harvests were profound. Most directly, there were extensive employment declines in the timber industry and a number of timber-related businesses were forced to close (Sherman 2006, 2009). Numerous individuals who had worked in the timber industry their entire life and had developed skills enabling them to make a comfortable living working in the forests lost their jobs. Most of these workers lacked skills that would enable them to obtain high-quality employment in another sector. Thus, these individuals were left with two options, neither of which was very appealing. They could leave town and seek work elsewhere or remain in their hometown and obtain a lower-paying job, often in the service sector.

Economic implications soon extended beyond timber workers and timber-related businesses. As employment levels continued to decline, and as many remaining workers had less income, a number of businesses not directly

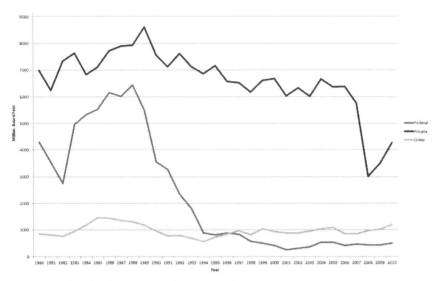

**FIGURE 5.2.** Timber harvest, Washington and Oregon, 1980–2010

involved in the timber industry began to falter. City and county tax revenues consequently shriveled, which significantly affected the ability of communities to support schools and provide other public services. Job losses and income declines also placed considerable stress on marriages and families (Sherman 2005, 2006, 2009).

An added problem was the loss of timber-related federal revenues to cities and counties. Local and state governments have never been able to get property tax revenues from federally owned land, which is a significant concern because so much of the land in the west is federally owned. However, throughout most of the twentieth century, federal laws allowed county governments to receive 25 percent of the revenue generated from timber, grazing, or mining leases on Forest Service and other federal land. These funds are called payment in lieu of taxes (PILT). Many counties in Washington, Oregon, and other western states with significant timber industries had become dependent on these funds to provide for local school and other government services. As the amount of logging on federal land declined, these revenues regressed as well. For example, Oregon's Lake County received $5.3 million a year in federal timber revenue in 1987 and 1988. In 1998, the county collected only $300,000 (LeMonds 2001).

*Forks, Washington*

Forks, Washington, was once the prototypical logging community. When driving into Forks in the 1980s, one was greeted with a sign stating, "Welcome to Forks, Logging Capitol of the World." Forks is located on Washington's western peninsula, where extensive rainfall makes the area the epitome of northwest forests. Forks averages about 107 inches of precipitation annually and has 212 days per year with measurable precipitation. On days when the sun shines, the scenery is spectacular. On one side is the rugged Pacific Coast, and on the other are the snow-covered peaks of Olympic National Park. The national park is like the hole of a donut and while much of the park consists of snow-covered peaks, considerable amounts of old-growth forests are found within park boundaries. Surrounding the national park are heavily wooded areas owned by a combination of the federal government (US Forest Service and BLM), state, tribal, and privately owned lands.

The location of Forks on the rugged peninsula resulted in much later settlement and later development of the timber industry compared to other parts of the state and region. While trees were abundant, extreme isolation made it difficult to get timber to market. At the conclusion of World War II, improved roads funded by federal and state governments were built into the region, and the timber industry exploded. As a consequence, the population of Clallam County (where Forks is located) nearly doubled from 30,022 in 1960 to 56,464 in 1990 (figure 5.3). The timber industry reached its peak in Clallam County in 1986 with the harvest of 445 million board feet of timber. As with the rest of the northwest region, timber harvests declined sharply resulting from spotted owl rulings beginning in about 1990. In 1994, 164 million board feet of timber were harvested in the county, only 37 percent as much as just a few years earlier. Harvests were further reduced to 142 million board feet in 2009 during the Great Recession. As with the rest of the region, declines were especially pronounced on federal land. In 1986, 31.5 percent of Clallam County timber harvest was from federal land. By 1994, this proportion had been reduced to less than 1 percent (figure 5.4).

The implications of timber harvest reductions in Forks were similar to what happened in the rest of the region. Jobs were lost, businesses were closed, and many people were forced to migrate from the community. Public revenues diminished, and many marriages and families were severely stressed.

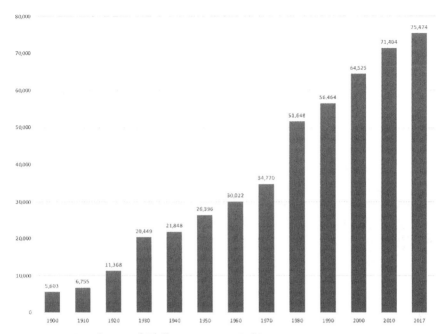

**FIGURE 5.3.** Population of Clallam County, Washington, 1900–2017

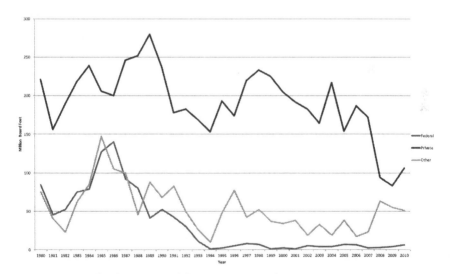

**FIGURE 5.4.** Timber harvest in Clallam County, Washington, 1980–2010

The transition from a dependence on logging to dependence on something else was extremely difficult both economically and culturally and took years to achieve.

Forks is now a very different community than it was during the 1980s. It still rains extensively, it is still very green, and there are still lots of trees, but Forks is no longer heavily dependent on the timber industry. The sign stating that Forks is the logging capitol of the world no longer stands. Like many other communities in the Northwest, Forks has advantages that made the transition a little easier. Forks is located in a high-amenity region, and being next to Olympic National Park enhances this advantage. Consequently, the tourism industry has flourished in recent years.

The tourism industry has an added advantage in that Stephenie Meyer chose Forks as the location for her popular Twilight book series; the books have sold more than 100 million copies worldwide. Ms. Meyer had never been to Forks prior to writing her books, but she wanted a place that was dark and dreary as befits vampires. The rain consistently rolling in from the Pacific seemed to make Forks the ideal spot. Regardless of the reason the community was chosen, Forks is able to use Twilight publicity to attract even more tourists. While jobs in the tourism sector are better than no jobs at all, a major problem experienced by Forks and other former timber communities able to generate a tourist industry is that many tourism jobs are low wage, are seasonal, and fail to replace the much-higher-paying jobs that were lost with timber industry declines. As a consequence, according to the US Census, the median income in Clallam County was $47,180 in 2012–16 compared to $62,848 for the state of Washington.

In a strongly Democrat state, the voters of Clallam County chose Donald Trump (46.4%) in a close vote over Hillary Clinton (43.6%) in 2016. Clallam County voted for President Obama in both 2008 and 2012.

## The Future of Timber Communities

The vast forests of the Pacific Northwest were harvested unsustainably for decades. The battle over the spotted owl was really a battle over the preservation of segments of old-growth forest. The consequence of extremely antagonistic battles was that timber harvests were greatly reduced and that pockets of old growth timber were preserved. At the same time, thousands of jobs were lost, marriages and families were stressed, and communities struggled. Despite these changes, spotted owl numbers continue to decline.

Even legislative changes that removed protection for the spotted owl would not bring back the logging industry as it existed previously. First, continued improvement in logging technology has steadily reduced the need for timber workers. A single worker with modern machinery can produce more timber in a day than a large crew could produce in a month in previous eras. In the western United States combined, the number of workers in the logging industry in 2017 was only about one-third as many as in 1990. Second, demand for timber has declined in recent years. Demand for paper has declined considerably as a result of modern technology whereby messages are sent and data stored electronically. Further, the demand for wood in the construction industry has declined because the use of other materials has increased.

Like rural communities everywhere, the path for Forks and other former timber-dependent communities to economic and demographic stability is to fully embrace modern information and communication technology and develop a twenty-first-century information and knowledge economy as will be described in chapter 10.

# 6

## Mineral Development

The quest for minerals played a vital role in the settlement and initial development of the West. In scattered locations, discoveries of gold, silver, copper, lead, zinc, and other minerals were the impetus for thousands of people to move to the West. Billions of dollars' worth of minerals have been extracted from western mines, and some individuals have earned vast fortunes. Where minerals were discovered, communities emerged. Many modern western communities had their beginnings as mining towns. Communities that began as mining towns include state capitols such as Denver, Colorado; Helena, Montana; and Carson City, Nevada. Several major resort communities such as Aspen and Telluride, Colorado, and Park City, Utah, also began as mining towns. Many other former mining towns have become ghost towns.

Both environmental and economic problems have accompanied mineral development from the beginning. Prominently, severe environmental problems are a lasting legacy of most mining ventures. By definition, mining is not sustainable. Minerals developed through geologic time, and when these minerals are removed, they can't be replaced. Also, by its very nature, mining is

DOI: 10.7330/9781607329510.c006

environmentally disruptive. Minerals are typically underground, and soil and rock must be removed or tunnels dug to reach them. Further, valuable minerals generally are only a small proportion of the rocks and soil within which they are found. The ore removed in a high-quality copper mine, for example, typically contains less than 1 percent copper (Carter 2012; Rosenblum 1995). The valuable ore must be separated from other material, a process that sometimes involves the use of acids and other chemicals or a smelting process to burn off the unwanted materials. Tailings that remain after the minerals have been removed represent a substantial hazard, as they are often laced with poisonous acids, chemicals, or heavy metals, all of which tend to be washed or leached into nearby water supplies and can have disastrous consequences (Stiller 2000). The air pollution resulting from the smelting process is another significant problem.

Early miners largely ignored environmental problems, and thus we are left to cope with them today. Often a dam is built to prevent these dangerous materials from washing into streams and rivers while attempts to remove them are undertaken. Evidence of the environmental dangers posed by mining was again apparent during the summer of 2015. On August 5, Environmental Protection Agency (EPA) contractors inadvertently broke a plug holding contaminated water in abandoned mining tunnels from the Gold King Mine near Silverton, Colorado. Three million gallons of contaminated water escaped. The Gold King Mine was a Superfund Site; the EPA was attempting to cope with pollution problems resulting from a mine that has been closed for decades. The contaminated water contained high levels of heavy metals such as lead and arsenic. When the contaminated water reached the Animas River, the river was turned to a sickly orange/yellow color (Weiser 2018). The yellow water then ran into the San Juan River, which flows through the Navajo Reservation in northern New Mexico. San Juan River water is critical for irrigation and other purposes all along its length. At the peak of the agricultural growing season, farmers were unable to irrigate because their water supply was contaminated, which had dramatic consequences for crop production and family incomes.

Heavy metals do not vanish or disappear when they wash downstream. Rather, they are simply diluted as when the San Juan River flowed into Lake Powell and merged with the Colorado River. From Lake Powell, the contaminated water ran through Grand Canyon and into Lake Mead. From Lake

Mead, the water is used extensively in Arizona and California for agriculture and municipal purposes. While the pollution was diluted enough that the water was no longer yellow, there is no question that the contaminants remained and presented danger to everyone who used the water. It should be remembered that there are literally thousands of abandoned mines like the Gold King scattered across the west.

In addition to facing environmental problems, communities dependent on natural resource extraction have always underperformed economically. This phenomenon is known as the "natural resource curse" and has been observed throughout the world and at every level of geography—nations, states, and local communities—and was discussed in chapter 4 (Van der Ploeg and Venables 2012; Weinstein and Partridge 2014). Further, mining communities have always struggled with cycles of boom and bust. When minerals are discovered, people move to the area for employment or to seek their fortune. Businesses then emerge to provide services to miners and others involved in mineral industries. Often the growth is rapid, and some individuals do extremely well financially. Later, when minerals are depleted, the residents leave and businesses are forced to close. As a result, numerous former mining communities that are now ghost towns or near ghost towns are scattered across the west.

The demand for minerals remains high. Minerals are vital in many of the products that define our twenty-first-century world such as computers, cell phones, televisions, planes, and cars. Consider the example of copper. Copper does not rust or decay, it is easily malleable and thus can be used for a wide range of products, and it is easy to recycle. Copper is used for the thousands of miles of electrical wiring across this and other countries. About 400 pounds of copper wire are used in the average home's electrical wiring and plumbing. Televisions, radios, dishwashers, and dryers all use copper. Copper is also used extensively in pipes and hoses. The average car has about 40 pounds of copper, primarily in the battery and other electrical wiring components. A Toyota Prius has more because of the automobile's more complex batteries. Each of the billions of cell phones is dependent upon copper. Our twenty-first-century way of life would be impossible without copper (Carter 2012). The problem is we have not devised a way to obtain copper without major environmental disruptions.

From a community development perspective, the goal in mineral extraction is to enhance the positive (jobs, incomes, and provision of essential resources) while limiting the negative (environmental problems, economic underperformance and the boom-bust cycle). In this chapter, we utilize mining communities in Montana and Arizona as examples of what has happened in the past and explore possible approaches for moving forward in a more efficient manner in the future.

## Mining in Montana and Arizona

On January 24, 1848, gold was discovered at Sutter's Mill along the American River in California. When word of this discovery reached the eastern United States, it led to the California Gold Rush of 1849 when thousands of people crossed the continent seeking wealth. Later, gold was discovered at Pikes Peak in Colorado and silver at Comstock Lode in Nevada (Stiller 2000). Boomtowns sprouted up around these and many other mineral strikes throughout the West.

Among the most significant mineral discoveries in the nineteenth-century West were those occurring in Montana. On July 28, 1862, gold was discovered at Grasshopper Creek in what is now southwest Montana. Very quickly the town of Bannack emerged, becoming Montana's first mining boomtown. Initially, the town was nothing but tents scattered across the prairie. Early residents were mostly men and included drifters, persons running from the law, defectors from Civil War armies, and others looking for a new start. Only a few women lived in Bannack in the early days, and many of them were sex workers. Isolation was extreme because there was not another community in any direction for at least 400 miles.

A few months after the Bannack strike, a group of prospectors discovered more gold near Alder Creek, about seventy-five miles east of Bannack. Within weeks, another mining boomtown emerged, with the center of this boom located at Virginia City. As can be imagined, Bannack and Virginia City fit the definition of the lawless, Wild West. With a total lack of legitimate law, drinking, gambling, fighting, and prostitution were rampant. In Bannack, the sheriff was hung by a vigilante committee when it was learned that he was involved in a scheme to steal gold as it was being shipped to market.

As is often the case in mining, the gold fields of Bannack and Virginia City soon played out. Bannack is now a ghost town, and in 2010 Virginia City had a population of only 190. Minerals, however, were discovered in other parts of the state. For example, important resources were found in Helena, and that mining boomtown eventually became the state capital.

One of the first miners to arrive in Bannack was William Andrews Clark. Clark had been born in Pennsylvania in 1839 and went west to work in the Colorado mines in 1862. During his first year of mining in Montana, he worked hard and found a substantial amount of gold. When winter set in, most of the miners spent their earnings on alcohol and prostitutes. Clark, instead, purchased a wagon and team and traveled over terrible roads and winter conditions for 400 miles to Salt Lake City. In Salt Lake City, he purchased goods that were in short supply and would be valuable in the mining camps. He then traveled the 400 miles back to Montana and sold his goods at considerable profit. Clark realized he could make much more money providing services to the miners than he could by actually working in the mines. From that point on, he engaged in providing a variety of services and supplies to mining communities throughout Montana. As other mining boomtowns emerged, Clark would develop businesses to provide services to these isolated mining towns. He then started owning and managing the mines. In time, Clark became one of the wealthier people in the country.

*The Richest Hill on Earth*

In the 1870s, gold, silver, and copper were found in a hill near what is now Butte, Montana. Early miners, however, struggled to make Butte area mining profitable. The amount of minerals per volume of ore was too low for individual miners to turn a significant profit. Further, the mines were producing a variety of minerals (gold, silver, and copper) that made the mines more difficult to work. During this time, William Andrews Clark moved to Butte, where he established a bank and then invested in area mines and businesses. Another entrepreneur, Marcus Daly, developed some mines and built a smelter and refinery nearby that helped improve the profitability of the mines. The town of Anaconda grew up around Daly's refinery.

Very quickly, the amount of gold and silver being obtained from Butte mines began to decline. As this occurred, many miners became discouraged and moved away. As gold and silver declined, however, the amount of copper being recovered increased. Individuals such as Clark and Daly recognized the potential for copper. In the 1800s, copper mining was very different from mining precious metals such as gold and silver. With precious metals, an individual on their own had a chance of doing reasonably well, as even a small amount of the metal was extremely valuable. Mining base metals such as copper is very different because its per-ounce value is much lower. Thus, from the beginning, base metal mining was much more conducive to corporate mining using big machines and a large paid workforce. The availability of a refinery was also essential to make copper profitable, something beyond the capacity of all but very wealthy individuals.

Butte mines were helped because in the later decades of the 1800s, demand for copper was skyrocketing. Prior to the late nineteenth century, copper had been used for pots and pans, for utensils, for art, and for a sheath on ships to prevent the wood from rotting. When Columbus sailed to the Americas, his ships were sheathed in copper. In addition, for centuries copper had been mixed with tin to make bronze. By the late 1800s, telegraph lines were crossing the country, and demand for electrical wiring was growing as more homes and businesses obtained electricity. Copper was the primary element in telegraph and electrical wiring.

Clark, Daly, and a few others quickly gained control of Butte mines and together became known as the "Copper Kings." In time, the wealth extracted from Butte mines made the Copper Kings among the richest people in the world. The hill where mines were being developed became known as the "richest hill on earth" (Hyde 1998).

As production increased, demand for miners grew and thus the population of Butte exploded. Miners came from around the world to work in the mines, and in the early days of Butte a high proportion of community residents were foreign born. By 1890 there were 24,000 residents in the community and in 1920 the population exceeded 60,000, making Butte one of the largest cities in the intermountain West (see figure 6.1 for population of Silver Bow County).

During the early years, Butte experienced most of the issues and problems common to mining towns. Most miners were young and single men, and after a long shift in dark and damp mines, they were ready for a break and some excitement. Hundreds of salons lined the streets of Butte, and drunkenness and fights were commonplace. There was an extensive red-light district.

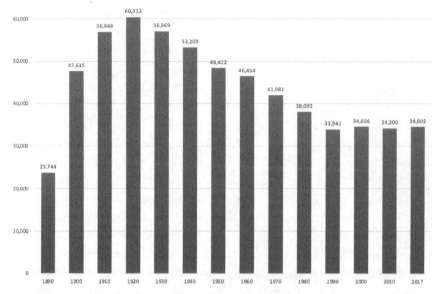

**FIGURE 6.1.** Population of Silver Bow County, Montana, 1890–2017

Further, mining was an extremely dangerous occupation, and many accidents resulted in the injury or even death of individuals. Miners were killed and injured by mine cave-ins, by fire, by getting run over by ore trains, by malfunctions of the cage that dropped them deep in to mines, and in numerous other ways. Many of those who were not killed in accidents had their lifespan reduced by miner's lung (pneumoconiosis) that is caused by the inhalation of dust in mines. Some large-scale accidents also occurred in the Butte area. The worst was an accident on June 8, 1917, when a cave-in occurred at the Granite Mountain Mine that resulted in the death of 168 miners.

Butte also has a long history of labor disputes. The first labor union in Butte was organized in 1878, shortly after mining began. Through unions, miners were seeking better wages, shorter hours, and safer working conditions. Mine owners and management, led by the Copper Kings, did their best to weaken the unions, which would allow the owners to keep costs lower so they could make a greater profit. Because of the large number of mine workers and the strength of the unions, Montana was a strong Democrat state in that era. As a measure of the strength of organized labor, in 1911 and again in 1913, Louis Duncan, a member of the Socialist Party of America, was elected mayor of Butte.

An important page in the history of organized labor in Butte happened in 1920. That year, the Industrial Workers of the World (IWW) called a strike. Typical of other labor disputes, the workers wanted higher wages, an eight-hour workday, safer conditions, and an end of the "rustling card." Through the rustling card system, employers blacklisted persons involved in union organizing. On April 21, 1920, company guards fired upon striking miners who were picketing. One person was killed and sixteen were injured, an action that became known as the Anaconda Road Massacre. No one was ever punished for the death and the injuries.

The Copper Kings were accused of exploiting their workers and attempting to control the political system in order to keep their wealth accruing. They also battled one another in an attempt for complete control, a battle that spilled over into politics. In 1888, Clark ran for the position of territorial delegate to congress as a Democrat. At that time, Montana was a heavily Democratic state and Clark should have won easily. However, he lost by over 5,000 votes. It was found out later that Daly had pressured his employees to vote for Clark's Republican opponent.

Montana became a state in 1889, and in 1899 Clark was elected senator from Montana. This was a time when senators were elected by their state legislatures. It was later determined that Clark had bribed state senators for their vote—sometimes up to $10,000 per vote. Aware of the bribery, the US Senate then refused to seat Clark. These actions were a critical factor in the later passage of the seventeenth amendment that resulted in senators being elected by popular vote. Clark was again elected senator in 1901 and served one term, until 1907.

Utilizing his wealth, Clark later became involved in the railroad industry. The city of Las Vegas, Nevada, was established as a railroad stop on a rail route Clark built between Los Angeles and Salt Lake City. Las Vegas is in Clark County, which is named in honor of William Andrews Clark because he chose to have his railroad pass through this county.

Montana politics make it apparent that extensive power emanates from great wealth. In a 1907 essay on Clark, Mark Twain stated, "He is as rotten a human being as can be found anywhere under the flag; he is a shame to the American nation, and no one has helped to send him to the Senate who did not know that his proper place was the penitentiary, with a ball and chain on his legs."

## The Decline of Butte

Copper extraction reached a peak in Butte in about 1920 and gradually declined thereafter. Copper demand declined temporally after World War I and through the Great Depression, which resulted in lower prices. Additionally, copper in the Butte mines was being depleted. Consequently, Butte output was unable to keep pace with more productive mines in other parts of the world such as Arizona and Chile. In the 1950s, in an attempt to keep the mines in operation, the decision was made to switch from the more costly and dangerous underground mining to open-pit mining. By the 1980s, the quality of ore had declined to the point that even open-pit mining was no longer profitable, and all of the Butte area mines were closed.

In the past three decades, Butte has confronted several major problems from being a declining mining town. An obvious concern is economic decline. As copper production dwindled and as open-pit mines replaced underground mines, fewer miners were needed. This problem was confounded when even the open-pit mines were closed. There was no way for Butte to replace the thousands of relatively high-paying jobs in the mines. With fewer miners, the businesses serving miners began to stumble, and many of them were forced to close. Under these circumstances, the community had trouble providing basic services such as schools. By 2010, the population of Silver Bow County, where Butte is located, was only 34,200, barely half of what it had been in 1920 (figure 6.1).

Another lasting legacy of a century of mining is severe environmental problems. Resulting from problems in Butte and other mining communities, the Comprehensive Environmental Response, Compensation, and Liability Act (CERCLA) was passed in 1980. This law (commonly referred to as Superfund) requires the EPA to clean up and alleviate problems resulting from toxic waste sites that threaten human health. It is necessary for the federal government to get involved because the mining companies often declare bankruptcy and thus fail to clean up the mess they created. The most expensive Superfund site in history is the Butte/Anaconda region of Montana. Coping with such profound economic and environmental issues is obviously overwhelming to Butte/Anaconda residents.

Most of the residents of Butte have accepted the fact that the mining industry is not coming back and that they will have to look elsewhere to rebuild their economy. This process has been more complex because of the environmental damage left by a century of mining. A careful examination of community assets and liabilities and an understanding of the modern economy have resulted in efforts that have led to the rebuilding of downtown Butte. This revitalization has attracted businesses bringing employment opportunities that can be successful in the modern world and that match the job skills of the local workforce. While the economy is not as dynamic as it was during the height of the mining boom, the community is again economically and demographically stable. For former mining communities, this stability is probably the best that could be hoped for. Approaches utilized in Butte in recent years should be duplicated in other mining communities. Of course, rather than waiting 100 years and experiencing extensive environmental and economic disruptions, this process of incorporating balance among environmental and economic concerns should begin when mining begins. Perhaps because the residents of Butte recognize that their future is in industries other than mining, Silver Bow County consistently votes Democrat and did so again in the 2016 election.

## Mining in Arizona

Late in the nineteenth century, a variety of minerals were discovered at several locations throughout southeast Arizona and southwest New Mexico. As with mineral strikes everywhere, many people moved to the area seeking riches. Among the early immigrants to southeast Arizona in search of wealth were Wyatt Earp, his brothers, and their friend Doc Holliday, famous for their involvement in the well-known "Gunfight at the OK Corral" in Tombstone, Arizona.

Arizona mining efforts soon concentrated on copper, which was found in great abundance. Arizona mines have a greater proportion of copper than anywhere else in the United States. Only in Chile are copper resources found in greater abundance than in Arizona. Soon major mines were operating in several Arizona locations, including Bisbee and Morenci. As in Montana, copper mining in Arizona involved major companies with a large hired workforce. The Morenci Mine (figure 6.2), in Greenlee County, has been the most productive copper mine in US history and continues to produce large amounts of the metal. In 2013, 1.22 million tons of copper,

**FIGURE 6.2.** Morenci Mine (istockphoto.com)

valued at over $9 billion, was mined in the United States. More than 99 percent of this copper was mined in the West, with 60 percent of US copper produced coming from Arizona.

At the Morenci Mine, a company town (named Morenci) was built at the edge of the operations. Like all company towns, the company (originally Phelps Dodge and now Freeport-McMoRan) owns all of the homes, businesses, and schools in the community. Mine employees can rent a home in Morenci but must move out if their employment at the mines comes to an end. People who chose not to live in a company town can live a few miles down the road in Clifton, where it is possible to own one's own home or business. Figure 6.3 shows population trends in Greenlee County.

The Arizona mines have struggled with the same issues that have plagued mines everywhere. In Arizona mines, these issues are compounded by racial strife. In the late nineteenth century, executives at the Morenci Mine recruited workers from nearby Mexico, as they needed a large, unskilled labor force. In 1917, 80 percent of the Morenci Mine labor force was Latinx. An added benefit for the company of recruiting workers from Mexico is that in the early days it could pay Latinx workers less than white workers. At one point, white workers were listed as "miners" and were paid thirty-three dollars per week; Latinxs were listed as "laborers" and were paid nineteen dollars per week. At this time, there was no chance for a Latinx worker to advance beyond being a laborer. A Mexican worker who touched a locomotive would be fired on the spot. Additionally, until the 1960s segregation in

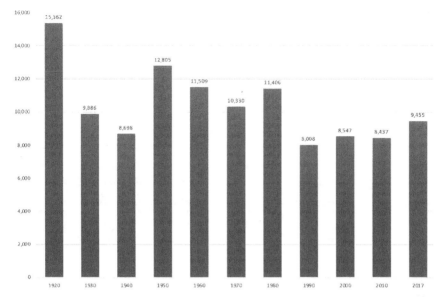

**FIGURE 6.3.** Population of Greenlee County, Arizona, 1920–2017

Morenci was complete, Latinx and white workers had separate locker rooms at the job site, they lived in separate sections of Morenci, and their children attended separate schools. In contrast to Morenci, the Bisbee mines were underground and needed a more skilled labor force. They hired nearly all white workers (Kingsolver 1989).

The racial strife in Morenci is exemplified by an event that occurred in 1904. A local Catholic church, which many of the Latinxs attended, made arrangements with a Catholic orphanage in New York City to adopt about forty children. Each of the adoptive families went through a screening process and was approved. Three nuns from the orphanage traveled by train with the children from New York to Arizona. As the children were getting off of the train, local leaders were stunned to see that the children were white. The decision was made that they couldn't allow these white children to live in Latinx homes. Local police were sent from house to house to gather all of the children who had recently arrived from New York. Some of the children were then placed with white families, while the remaining children were returned to New York. This case was taken to court and eventually reached the Supreme Court. The Supreme Court refused to hear the case, meaning the decision of the lower court stood. The lower court decision was that city officials and law enforcement were justified in removing the children from their new adoptive homes (Carter 2012).

Conflict between labor and management has been a constant theme in the Morenci mines. Mother Jones visited Arizona to help organize labor unions just prior to US entry into World War I. Barely five feet tall; Mother Jones was a tireless fighter for workers' rights. Her approach differed from most labor organizers of the time in that she welcomed minorities and women and fought for the rights of children. In 1915, the union called a strike and was successful in obtaining higher wages and improved working conditions. Mine owners (Phelps Dodge) then fought back. On July 12, 1917, 1,200 union workers were rounded up at gunpoint as they arrived at work. Those who wouldn't swear allegiance to the company were loaded onto the boxcars of a train and shipped to New Mexico. Few of the worker sent away on the train ever returned to Morenci.

More recently, a 1983 strike at the Morenci Mine is said to have significantly impacted all labor unions in the United States ever since. This strike began at midnight on June 30, 1983. At the time, most workers expected this strike to be similar to the others and to be over in a couple of weeks. Phelps Dodge (the mine owner), however, was convinced that the time was right to break the union for good. The fact that there was an antiunion president in the White House, Ronald Reagan, at the time emboldened the company. Reagan had just made his views on unions apparent when he fired all of the air traffic controllers during their strike.

When union miners walked off the job at the beginning of the strike, Phelps Dodge remained committed to keep the mine running. To do this, the company had some managers work in the mine, they encouraged union miners to cross the picket line by providing financial bonuses to those who did, and they hired replacement workers. For decades following the strike, strong feelings persisted between persons who crossed the picket line and those who did not. Circumstances in town became extremely tense after a couple of weeks without paychecks. Without a paycheck, bills didn't get paid, cars were repossessed, and families were evicted from their homes. Tension grew as the mine kept running. One night a little girl was struck in the head by a bullet when a gun was fired into her family's house after the girl's father crossed the picket line to work. Eventually the union was broken. Some union workers never got their jobs back. Most replacement workers were able to retain their jobs on a permanent basis.

Following the 1983 Morenci strike, the practice of hiring replacement workers has become common practice. Since that time, union membership has plummeted and the power of unions has been greatly diminished. Prior to the strike, Greenlee County had always voted Democrat, since the Democrat Party supported policies to strengthen unions. Results were similar in other mining and industrial communities with a large unionized labor force. For example, FDR got 86.2 percent of the vote in Greenlee County in 1936. Since that time, the blue-collar vote has moved steadily to the Republican Party. The Republican presidential candidate has won in Greenlee County in each election since 2000. In 2016, Trump received 57.3 percent of the vote in Greenlee County. No question, Trump would have received an even higher proportion of the vote, but nearly one-half of the residents in the county were Latinxs. Latinx voters were much less likely to vote for Trump than were white voters.

## The Future of Mining Communities

With continued high demand for minerals, mining and all of its subsequent challenges will be with us into the foreseeable future. In 2013, 227 tons of gold was mined in the United States, valued at $10.2 billion. The United States produced 10 percent of the world's gold. Eighty percent of the gold produced in the United States now comes from the State of Nevada. The world's largest producer of gold was China followed by Australia and South Africa. The importance of copper and significance of the West in copper production have been previously described. A number of other minerals continue to be mined in the western United States.

As long as humans desire to use cell phones, computers, cars, and planes, there will be a demand for mineral resources. Consequently, mining is here to stay for at least the foreseeable future. At the same time, it is essential to recognize that mining is not sustainable and that eventually the mineral resources will be depleted. Mining, like all industries, will continue to become ever more mechanized. Administrators at the Morenci Mine believe that robots will conduct much of the mining in the future. As machines replace human labor, the number of jobs in mining will continue to decline. Developing stable, economically viable communities based on the mining industry is thus not a reasonable plan. While the resource base is available, communities should prepare for the day that the industry will end. When the economy is booming, efforts should be made to upgrade and modernize infrastructure. Alternative approaches for generating jobs and economic activity should be explored. In this regard, it is critical to develop a twenty-first-century economy based on information and knowledge.

# 7

## Amenity and Tourism Communities

The aesthetic beauty of some places is incredible. There is no question that such beauty can be used as a tool to spur economic development in the modern world. In the modern world, when more people are free to live where they chose, many choose to live in amenity-rich communities. A classic case in point, one of the most serenely beautiful views in the world is from the shores of Jackson Lake in Grand Teton National Park in Teton County, Wyoming (Albrecht 2014a). Behind the lake are the rugged peaks of the picturesque Teton Mountains, rising to an elevation of over 13,000 feet.

During the late 1800s when the West was being settled, the lack of available natural resources that could be used in the goods producing industries made it difficult to earn a living in the area, and thus the Teton area had few residents. The spectacular amenities made little difference in economic development efforts. Because the population was so small, Teton County was not even organized until the 1920s, when it was divided from Lincoln County. In 1930, the total population of Teton County was 2,003, with 307 residents living in the county seat of Jackson. Most of the population was striving to earn

DOI: 10.7330/9781607329510.c007

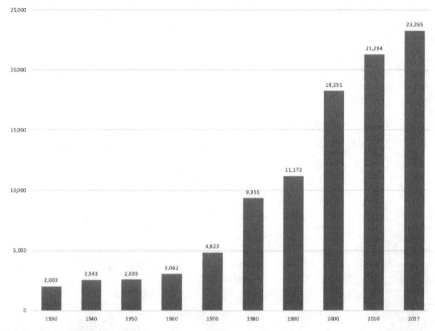

**FIGURE 7.1.** Population of Teton County, Wyoming, 1930–2017

a living from marginal ranching and farming operations. Crop production was especially difficult because the elevation of Jackson is 6,234 feet and the growing season is short.

Initial proposals to preserve the Teton Mountains as a National Park were met with strong local and statewide opposition because of concerns that this would have a negative impact on sheep grazing. Despite this opposition, Grand Teton National Park was created in 1929. Even with increased tourism that creation of the park generated, little economic or demographic development occurred for decades. The population of Teton County was only 2,543 in 1940; 2,503 in 1950; and 3,062 in 1960.

Transition from a ranching town to a resort community began rather innocuously in the late 1960s with development of two ski resorts. Evidence of growth and development resulting from the ski resorts was apparent as the county population increased to 4,823 in 1970. Eventually, skiing became a part of year-round tourism, and souvenir shops replaced feed and hardware stores. Then condominiums, rental units, and golf courses emerged.

Intended clientele of these establishments was not locals, but visitors and wealthy newcomers who were moving into the valley. Real estate developers realized the potential market and began subdividing ranches into lots where the rich and famous could build trophy homes with views of the mountains (Travis 2007). By 2016, the population of Teton County had soared to 23,191. That number would be much higher but home prices are exorbitant and space is scarce, as much land is publicly owned. Average home prices and median household incomes are among the highest in the nation.

The transition to a high-end amenity community had consequences in Teton County. Most longtime residents were no longer able to afford soaring housing prices and had to move unless they had made a fortune subdividing and selling their farm or ranch properties. As living costs skyrocketed, low-pay service workers, who are in great demand to care for wealthy residents and other visitors, could no longer afford to live in Jackson. Many service workers now live in Driggs, Idaho, and make the thirty-mile drive through a difficult mountain pass daily to work in Jackson. Some major resorts even run a shuttle bus back and forth from Driggs to Jackson to provide transportation for their workers. Schoolteachers and other professionals find it difficult to afford living in Jackson. The school district is typically forced to hire young, inexperienced, and single teachers just out of college. Several of these young teachers then share an apartment as a way to make the rent affordable. In a few years, however, these teachers often desire a family or different living arrangements and so take a job elsewhere where living costs are lower and where they can afford more typical housing arrangements. The school district is then forced to hire another batch of young and inexperienced teachers just out of college. The schools and especially the students suffer the consequences.

Similar scenarios are apparent in high-amenity communities in other places. Aspen, Colorado, was originally settled when silver was discovered in 1879. By 1891, Aspen was among the leading silver-producing communities in the world. The 1890 Census reported that Pitkin County (where Aspen is located) had a population of 8,929. Then the silver mines played out, and Aspen went into a tailspin. By 1900 the population was down to 7,020. The population continued to decline, and by 1930 there were only 1,770 residents in the county. Most residents were surviving on marginal ranching and farming operations. Following World War II, a ski resort was built in the area, and

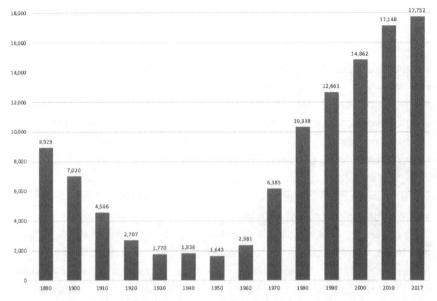

**FIGURE 7.2.** Population of Pitkin County, Colorado, 1890–2017

transition to a high-income resort community began. By 2017, the population of Pitkin County was 17,752, and the value of owner-occupied homes
was even higher than in Teton County, Wyoming (see figure 7.2). Many
long-time residents can no longer afford to live in Aspen, and many service
workers commute from Rifle, about sixty-eight miles away. Similar transitions have unfolded in other amenity-rich communities such as Breckenridge,
Steamboat Springs, and Telluride, Colorado, and Park City, Utah. Sun Valley,
Idaho, was built as a destination ski resort in the 1930s near what was then
the declining mining town of Ketchum. Vail, Colorado, was built as a resort
from the ground up. All of these communities are coping with extremely
high housing costs and the obstacles that these costs entail. Many other communities, to varying degrees, have utilized their amenities to attract residents
desiring to live in an amenity-rich destination. These communities are also
able to attract tourists in varying degrees.

    Along with experiencing higher housing and other costs, amenity com-
munities face additional obstacles to becoming economically stable and viable. Significantly, the tourism industry that blossoms in many amenity-rich

communities tends to generate jobs that are low pay and seasonal. Low pay levels make it difficult for people to hold tourism jobs long term, and many are eventually forced to seek employment in another sector. The problem of low pay is confounded by seasonality, which makes it necessary for many people holding tourism jobs to move elsewhere during the off-season. As a consequence, the tourism labor force is extremely unstable. Typically, the labor force is young people who have tourism jobs during the summer while attending college the rest of the year.

Another problem confronting many growing amenity communities is conflict between the newcomers and longtime residents. Research shows that these two groups of people often have very different values and attitudes about environmental and other issues (Smith and Krannich 2000). Further, there is a direct relationship between the level of tourism development and the presence of negative attitudes about the tourism sector by residents (Smith and Krannich 1998). As the number of tourists in an area increases, negative attitudes about tourism increase. In many cases, longtime residents are descendants of the people that originally settled the community. Typically, the family has been dependent on employment in the goods producing industries for generations. Family members' desire is for the community to remain like it has always been, which means a continued dependence on the goods producing industries. Thus, they support policies and politicians that favor resource development that support these industries (Gosnell and Abrams 2011; Winkler et al. 2007).

In contrast, newcomers generally moved to the area because of amenities, and thus they desire the preservation of these amenities. Consequently, they typically oppose the types of developments favored by longtime residents. The conflict is often compounded because the newcomers generally have higher levels of education, higher incomes, and may have different religious and political views. I have attended many meetings in rural amenity communities where the newcomers and longtime residents sit on opposite sides of the table and glare at one another.

It is typically very easy to determine the extent to which communities have made the transition to high-end amenity and tourism communities by looking at election results. Most rural communities have voted heavily Republican in recent elections. However, as counties increasingly make the transition to amenity communities, the proportion of Democrat votes increases. In the 2016 presidential election, the major amenity communities voted in favor of Hillary Clinton. Rural counties in the West won by Clinton include Teton County (Jackson), Wyoming; Pitkin County (Aspen), Colorado; Eagle County (Vail), Colorado; Summit County (Breckenridge), Colorado; San Miguel County (Telluride), Colorado; Blaine County (Sun Valley), Idaho; and Summit County (Park City), Utah.

To better understand the issues and concerns facing amenity and tourism communities, the experiences of Moab, Utah, and Kenai Peninsula Borough, Alaska, are described. In recent years, Moab has steadily been moving toward a high-end amenity community, and their experiences are somewhat typical of other amenity communities. Kenai Peninsula is less developed along this path but has incredible amenity resources and thus great opportunity.

### Moab, Utah

Moab is located in Grand County on the banks of the Colorado River in southeast Utah. The community was settled by Mormon pioneers in the late 1800s and was traditionally economically dependent on irrigated agriculture and livestock grazing. Because of extreme isolation, the community was never very large or economically vibrant. In 1930, the population of Grand County was 1,813. Twenty years later (in 1950) the population was still only 1,903 (figure 7.3).

In the 1950s, the Moab area was at the center of a major uranium boom. The essential fuel for the nuclear bombs developed during World War II is uranium. During the war, uranium was imported from Congo, as there were no known economically viable sources in the United States. Following the war, demand for uranium increased because of the need for Cold War bombs and the development of nuclear power plants to produce energy. Substantial efforts were then made to find domestic sources of this critical resource. Attention quickly focused on the Colorado Plateau in the Four Corners area of Utah, Colorado, Arizona, and New Mexico. In 1952, a significant uranium reserve was discovered near Moab. The reserve eventually produced millions of dollars' worth of high-grade uranium. Discoveries were made in other parts the region, and soon hundreds of prospectors were combing the Four Corners area looking for additional deposits. Several uranium-milling plants were built, and a growing workforce was employed in the mines and the mills.

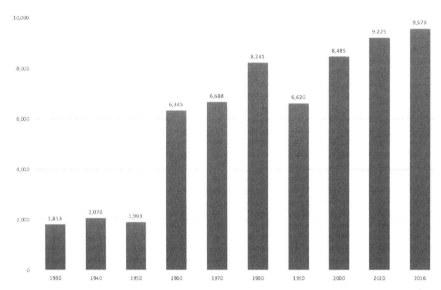

**FIGURE 7.3.** Total Population, Grand County, Utah, 1930–2016

Communities such as Moab, Utah, Grants, New Mexico, and Grand Junction, Colorado, experienced boomtown like growth throughout the 1950s. By 1960, the population of Moab had more than tripled to 6,345. In Grants, New Mexico, uranium development resulting in the population increasing from 2,251 in 1950 to 10,274 in 1960.

Then in 1960, the Atomic Energy Commission (the only legal buyer of uranium and uranium products) announced it had sufficient supplies. Prices plummeted, and uranium boomtowns experienced their bust. The economic downturn was compounded by severe environmental problems. Tailings from the uranium mine near Moab were stored in a pond near the Colorado River. It soon became apparent that radioactive tailings were leaching into the river and having disastrous effects on fish populations and other life. These tailings are now being transferred to a safer location as a part of a Superfund project at the cost of millions of taxpayer dollars.

The emergence of Moab as an amenity and tourism community began in the 1960s and early 1970s, when nearby Arches and Canyonlands were designated as National Parks after previously being National Monuments. It was at this time that Edward Abbey worked near Moab for a couple of summers and wrote his classic book *Desert Solitaire* (1968). The sheer red rock cliffs and natural sandstone arches provide a fabulously beautiful and unique landscape that soon began attracting vast numbers of tourists. A number of people also began moving to the area, desiring to live in an area with such extensive amenity and recreation opportunities.

Circumstances in Moab now resemble many amenity communities all over the country. New hotels and restaurants spring up each year, as do a variety of other businesses to serve the tourists. During summer months, the traffic is increasingly congested. Significantly, most of the jobs created by the tourism sector are low wage and seasonal. At the same time, there is strong demand for housing and so housing costs are high. The consequence is that in Grand County, average wages are well below the state average, but housing costs are significantly higher than the state average. This discrepancy is obviously a problem for many Moab residents. The number of tourists visiting during the summer is much larger than the number visiting during the winter, and so many workers are only employed seasonally. The community is seeking forms of employment that overcome the problems of low pay and seasonality. Some of these opportunities are described in chapter 10.

## Kenai Peninsula Borough, Alaska

The Kenai Peninsula is located just south of Anchorage, Alaska. Cook Inlet is located on the west side of the peninsula, while the Gulf of Alaska is on the east side. Like many other places in Alaska, Kenai Peninsula is blessed with incredible amenity resources that include towering mountains, glaciers, and active volcanoes. Wildlife includes bears, wolves, and moose, as well as abundant sea life such as whales, sea lions, and sea otters. Spectacular fishing for salmon and halibut is available. Commercial fishing is one of the area's most important industries.

In the 1950s a major oil reserve was discovered in Cook Inlet. Many believe the discovery of this oil reserve was significant in Alaska's becoming a state a few years later, as it now appeared that the new state could support itself financially. Very quickly, the oil industry became the most significant employer of Kenai Peninsula residents, and the population grew rapidly (figure 7.4). Over the years, production from this oilfield has declined

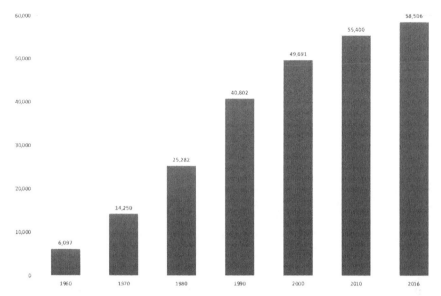

**FIGURE 7.4.** Total population, Kenai Peninsula Borough, Alaska, 1960–2016

as the resource has become depleted. As production from the Cook Inlet oilfield declined, construction of the Alaska pipeline to transport oil from Prudhoe Bay began. With the initiation of production from Alaska's north shore, Kenai Peninsula became an important bedroom community for this resource. Many individuals work a two-week shift on the north shore and then return to the Kenai Peninsula, where they spend their two weeks off. The worker's family typically lives on the Kenai Peninsula full time. Recently, serving as a bedroom community for the north shore has diminished as production from these oilfields has declined as the resource is depleted, which has resulted in reduced employment.

The Kenai Peninsula has a growing tourism community. People come from all over the world to fish for salmon and halibut and to view the glaciers and wildlife. Given the nature of the Alaskan climate, the problem of seasonality is especially severe. Like Moab, Kenai Peninsula needs year-round employment to help overcome the problems of declining energy employment and the seasonality and low wages of the tourism sector. Also, distance from major population centers negatively impacts the number of tourists to the area.

## The Future of Amenity and Tourism Communities

The significance of amenities and tourism is likely to increase in the years to come as travel becomes easier and more people are able to live where they wish rather than where their job is located. There are ways that amenity communities can use their aesthetic advantages to help achieve economic viability and stability. Attracting individuals who have stable, year-round jobs and who can live anywhere they choose can be very beneficial to amenity-based rural communities. These individuals provide assets and opportunities that help overcome the problems of seasonality and low pay that are typical of many jobs in amenity communities. These are the types of jobs described in chapter 10. Attracting these types of jobs can be one step in achieving economic diversity, which is a hallmark of economically viable communities.

# 8

# Federal Environmental Policies and Rural Economic Development

While attending a meeting with rural county commissioners in a western state, I listened to a speech by a member of the state legislature. He began by saying, "The biggest problem we face in the West is 'federal overreach.'" I hear this same sentiment over and over again when I visit rural communities in the West. What people mean by federal overreach is that federal policies and regulations (especially environmental regulations) have made it increasingly difficult for people to earn a living in the goods producing industries. What many people desire is a reduction in the amount of regulation. The notion of federal overreach was prominent in the support Trump received from rural voters in the 2016 election.

In earlier chapters of this book, examples emerged of federal policies that, at least to the views of rural residents, have interfered with their capacity to earn a living, especially in the goods producing industries. Many rural residents and other citizens believe the Endangered Species Act and the spotted owl ruling are what hurt the timber industry in the Pacific Northwest. Many believe that regulations to address climate change have crippled the coal

DOI: 10.7330/9781607329510.c008

industry. Some claim that air and water pollution control laws have encouraged manufacturing firms to move to other countries where environmental regulations are less stringent. In the West, many residents believe that federal land management policies have been harmful to the ranching and mining industries. Democrats generally support these pro-environmental policies. Partly as a consequence, rural counties most dependent on the goods producing industries tend to overwhelmingly vote for Republican candidates (Albrecht 2019).

A critical question is the extent to which these assertions are true. Do environmental regulations have negative implications for the economies of rural communities? To what extent are environmental regulations necessary? What policies would be most effective in helping communities build twenty-first-century economies based on information and knowledge? In this chapter and chapter 9, the relationship between federal policies and regulations, on the one hand, and rural economic development, on the other hand, is explored. In this current chapter, general environmental policies that impact the goods producing industries are explored. In chapter 9, federal land management policies and regulations are examined.

## Environmental Policies and Rural Economic Development

At one time, the development of resources to support the goods producing industries proceeded with little restraint. The first significant environmental regulations were a result of widespread concerns about the exploitation of resources on public land. The result was creation of the federal land management agencies to protect these resources. These actions are the topic of chapter 9.

Later, scientifically based ecological studies found that some resource uses were causing detrimental and sometimes irreparable damage to the environment and even to human health (Anderson et al. 2008). A watershed event was the publication of Rachel Carson's *Silent Spring* in 1962. Using careful scientific research, Carson noted negative environmental consequences resulting from the use of pesticides. Her insights included an explanation of how poisons become increasingly concentrated in body tissues as one moves up the food chain, causing genetic and reproductive disruption. Use of the pesticide DDT brought bald eagles to the verge of extinction and resulted in the banning of DDT. Since then, the eagles have made a remarkable comeback. Subsequent studies resulted in an improved understanding of the complexity of nature and knowledge that human actions can have unintended and sometimes irreparable negative consequences. The result was the birth of an environmental movement that placed pressure on policy makers to make changes to protect the environment.

These challenges culminated in the passage of several laws that forever ended the era of unfettered resource development without significant opposition and compromise. At this time support for environmental protection was bipartisan, and Republican president Richard Nixon signed many important policies into law. Among the most important of these laws from the Nixon and other administrations were the Clean Air Act of 1970, the Clean Water Act of 1972, the Wilderness Preservation Act of 1964, the National Wild and Scenic Rivers Act of 1968, the National Environmental Policy Act (NEPA) of 1969, the Endangered Species Act (ESA) of 1973, and the Federal Land Policy and Management Act (FLPMA) of 1976.

The Clean Air Act attempts to control both stationary and mobile sources of air pollution at the national level. The Clean Water Act limits both point and nonpoint pollution sources to retain the biological integrity of US water resources and wetlands. The Wilderness Preservation Act impacts management of federal land and is discussed in the next chapter. The National Wild and Scenic Rivers Act was intended to preserve free-flowing rivers with outstanding scenic, recreational, geological, fish and wildlife, historic, or cultural values. Rivers protected by this act are effectively off limits for dam construction. NEPA requires that environmental consequences of proposed federal actions be carefully analyzed before those actions take place. This analysis includes consideration of a wide range of species and more complex and longer-term environmental impacts. The ESA, administered by the US Fish and Wildlife Service, requires agencies to investigate whether species might be endangered or threatened as a consequence of human actions. If species are threatened or endangered, the US Fish and Wildlife Service is required to initiate action to prevent the continued decline of these species. ESA rulings were critical in the spotted owl controversy described in chapter 5. FLPMA was the culmination of combined efforts of environmental groups to widen the expressed purposes of public grazing lands managed by the BLM and authorizes consideration of recreational and wildlife interests in making range policy.

These policies were implemented to correct for market failures. Without regulation, companies can pollute the air and water. The companies receive the economic benefits of their actions, while everyone that breathes the air or uses the water shares the costs. The benefits of these environmental policies are unmistakable. Clean air and water mean that people are healthier and are able to live longer lives. Clean water and air result in healthier wildlife and unobstructed views. The quality of the air and of the water have both improved substantially since the passage of these regulations.

At the same time, concern is expressed about the extent to which these regulations have negative economic consequences. Opposition to environmental regulations initially emerged from those employed in the goods producing industries that were impacted by these new laws. This opposition was a factor leading to the election of Ronald Reagan in 1980. Reagan maintained that environmental regulations were a drag on the economy. His administration did its best to eliminate or weaken some environmental regulations, and it simply ignored other regulations. Since Reagan, environmental issues have become a significant partisan political issue, with Republicans consistently expressing support for resource development and Democrats placing emphasis on environmental protection.

In this chapter, two environmental protection issues and their rural economic development implications are described. The first issue relates to climate change, while the second concerns the possibility of the sage grouse being declared endangered under the ESA.

## Climate Change and Rural Economic Development

Scientists are virtually unanimous in their agreement that the earth's climate is changing and that these changes are largely a consequence of human activities, especially the burning of fossil fuels (e.g., Abatzoglou et al. 2014; Emanuel 2012; Giddens 2009; Houghton et al. 2001; IPCC 2014; Rahm 2010; Speth 2004; Washington and Cook 2011). Carbon Dioxide levels in the atmosphere, rising at an accelerating rate, have increased from about 280 part per million in preindustrial times to 411 in May of 2018. As of this writing, 2016 was the hottest year on record globally. This was the third year in a row that a new record for the hottest year ever had been established. Between 2000 and 2016, the earth has experienced sixteen of the seventeen hottest years on record. The last year the worldwide average temperature was below average was 1976.

Rising temperatures have consequences (Lachapelle and Albrecht 2019; Rosenzweig et al. 2008). Increasing ocean temperatures are leading to more frequent and more severe storms. During 2017, three historically devastating hurricanes (Harvey, Irma, and Maria) struck the United States and its territories causing extensive destruction. The much higher levels of carbon dioxide in the atmosphere are resulting in important chemical changes in oceans as they become more acidic. These changes are having major negative implications for coral reefs and other marine life. Forest fires in the West are becoming more frequent and severe. During summer months, a haze of smoke now covers much of the West.

In 2014, evidence emerged that the massive West Antarctic Ice Sheet has deteriorated to the point of no return as a result of warming temperatures and is gradually sliding into the sea. While this process may take decades, this event alone could raise the sea level by ten feet or more. Melting glaciers in other parts of the world, especially Greenland and Antarctica, are contributing to additional sea-level rises. Even a three-foot increase in sea level, which is small relative to changes that have occurred through earth's history, would displace around 100 million people.

Further, the extent of arctic snow cover has declined, and river flows have grown as the length of frost-free seasons has increased by as much as 50 percent. The permafrost is warming (Serreze et al. 2000), and its southern limit has moved north by a significant amount. As permafrost melts, the extensive amounts of methane, a potent GHG, that are released into the atmosphere contribute to even more severe climate change problems.

Human societies have become highly adapted to current climate conditions over millennia of relatively stable climate systems. Agriculture is finely tuned to present conditions; small shifts in temperature or precipitation could have dramatic and generally adverse consequences that could make feeding a growing human population ever more difficult (Emanuel 2012). Many species of living things are finely tuned to a specific environment, and even small climate changes could present serious obstacles to their continued survival.

Globally, the area affected by drought has increased since the 1970s. These changes make some habitats and some species extremely vulnerable (Allen-Diaz 1995; Emanuel 2012; IPCC 2014). The frequency and intensity of forest fires and insect disturbance have increased (Hassol 2004). For the most part, fire—and of relevance to this book—drought and other changes resulting from a changing climate place significant obstacles for those attempting to make a living in the goods producing industries such as farming, ranching, logging, and fishing.

The IPCC fifth assessment report (2014) concludes with high confidence that these changes are influenced by human activities. Likewise, the National Academy of Science has concurred with this assessment. If current trends continue, the amount of GHGs in the atmosphere will continue to grow, and the consequences could be disastrous (DiMento and Doughman 2014; Stern 2007).

While the dangers of climate change are apparent, efforts to address climate change issues have become vastly more difficult because climate change has become a partisan political issue. Views about climate change have had significant impacts on both local and national elections in recent years (Rahm 2010), and partisan politics makes attaining policies and programs to address growing concerns at both global and local levels much more difficult. During campaigns and as elected officials, Republicans are much more likely than Democrats to question the reality of climate change and to oppose policy efforts to address climate change concerns (Giddens 2009; McCright and Dunlap 2011a; Rahm 2010; Shearman and Smith 2007; Washington and Cook 2011), and the gap between the two parties is becoming progressively larger (Dunlap and McCright 2008).

Political polarization first became contentious with events surrounding the Kyoto Protocol. President Bill Clinton (a Democrat) supported United States involvement in international engagement on climate change, and the United States signed the treaty that was reached by the United Nations Framework Convention on Climate Change (UNFCCC) in Kyoto, Japan, on December 11, 1997 (hence the Kyoto Protocol). This treaty had the goal of stabilizing GHG concentrations in the atmosphere at a level that would prevent dangerous interference with climate systems.

At this point, a strong climate change denial campaign emerged in the United States (Brulle et al. 2012; Carmichael and Brulle 2017; McCright and Dunlap 2011b), with extensive financial support from groups that had a great deal to lose from policies intended to reduce fossil fuel consumption (Lahsen 2008; Mayer 2016; McCright 2007; McCright and Dunlap 2003; Oreskes and Conway 2008, 2010). The groups involved included in the denial campaign included the fossil fuel and other related industries (Freudenburg et al. 2008; Lahsen 2005; Layzer 2007), conservative think tanks, talk show hosts (McCright and Dunlap 2000, 2003; Oreskes and Conway 2008, 2010), and conservative Republican politicians (McCright and Dunlap 2003, 2000; Oreskes and Conway 2010). Strong statements by prominent Republican officials were an important part of the denial campaign. For example, Senator James Inhofe (Republican–Oklahoma) stated that climate change is "the greatest hoax ever perpetrated on the American people," and speaker of the house John Boehner (Republican–Ohio) pointed out that the idea that carbon dioxide is "harmful to the environment is almost comical." Right-wing talk show hosts tell their millions of listeners not only that climate change is a hoax, but that scientists are colluding to deceive them. Rush Limbaugh has stated that science is one of the four pillars of deceit. The other three are academia, government, and the media.

The goal of the climate change denial campaign was to create confusion and uncertainty about science in general and climate science in particular. In many ways, these efforts succeeded. Climate denial efforts were sufficient to erode both congressional endorsement and support from the general public. When President Clinton realized that he lacked sufficient support in Congress, the Kyoto Protocol was never submitted for ratification. Shortly after taking office, Republican president George W. Bush withdrew United States support for the protocol and refused to submit it to congress (Rahm 2010). As of 2013, 192 parties had ratified the protocol, and the United States was the only signatory not to have ratified it.

In December 2015, the UNFCCC submitted the Paris Agreement, an updated treaty to address climate change concerns. The primary goal of the Paris Agreement was to reduce GHG emissions to the point that global temperatures would not rise more than two degrees Celsius above preindustrial levels during the twenty-first century. At the time of the agreement, with support from the Obama administration, the United States was a full participant. Then on June 1, 2017, President Trump announced the United States was dropping out of the Paris Agreement, citing potential negative economic consequences. In late 2017, Nicaragua and Syria announced they were becoming participants in the Paris Agreement. This means that as of this writing, the United States is the only country in the world that is not a part of the Paris Agreement.

Withdrawals from both the Kyoto Protocol by the Bush administration and the Paris Agreement by the Trump administration were accompanied by denial rhetoric along with arguments that reducing carbon emissions would have harmful consequences for the economy. The heart of the denial campaign was to call into question the science behind climate change and make it seem as if there is extensive disagreement among climate scientists when in fact there is not (DiMento and Doughman 2014; Oreskes and Conway 2010; Powell 2011). A. Leiserowitz et al. (2017) found, for example, that only a small proportion of the American people realize that there is near-complete scientific consensus on the reality of climate change. This same process of denial and confusion has been used in other countries, such as Australia (Hamilton 2007), and on other issues including the health consequences of tobacco use, lead in gasoline, acid rain, and ozone depletion (Oreskes and Conway 2010).

A common, two-part argument of the climate denial community is (1) climate change has occurred throughout history, and (2) evidence that current climate changes are a function of human actions is insufficient. The scientific community's response is that while changing climate has been a constant in earth's history, the extent of change occurring in the past couple of decades exceeds what typically happens naturally over centuries or millennia. The extent and speed of changes that have already occurred and are projected for the future are occurring at unprecedented speed (Emanuel 2012).

The nature of climate change makes it a prime target for confusion among the general public, specifically along following lines: (1) Climate science is admittedly complex and uses concepts not readily understood by the general public such as probability and likelihood (Hulme 2009). (2) Climate change is not easy to observe at the local level. In contrast, if the local river is polluted or a layer of smog is hanging over one's hometown, it is more difficult to ignore. (3) The impacts of climate change are global. Thus, events occurring in China have significant implications for the future of polar bears in Alaska. Addressing climate change concerns is thus more difficult than dealing with localized issues (Speth 2004). (4) Most of the major consequences of climate change are in the future, which makes it easier to put off actions in order to deal with more immediately pressing concerns such as jobs and the economy. This point is especially true if people believe that policies to address climate change will have harmful implications for the economy (Washington and Cook 2011). (5) Finally, discussions of the impacts of climate change often appear catastrophic.

The result is often feelings of helplessness, since addressing climate change concerns is so difficult; a common response is to ignore or deny the problem. Under these circumstances, it is very easy for a confused public to look to their political or "thought leaders" for cues about what to believe and how to respond to climate change, and many people are comforted with thoughts that the problem is not real or at least not as bad as some say.

Hope exists because efforts to address significant worldwide environmental problems have occurred successfully in the past. For example, in 1985, scientists discovered that ozone in the stratosphere was being depleted. Of particular concern was a growing hole in the ozone over Antarctica. Depletion was a concern because ozone provides a shield from harmful ultraviolet radiation emitted by the sun. The major culprit leading to ozone depletion was emission of chlorofluorocarbons (CFCs), which were heavily used in advanced industrial nations as coolants for air conditioners and refrigerators and in aerosol cans. Representatives from nations around the world met in Montreal and agreed to ban usage of CFCs. This action became known as the Montreal Protocol. Industry quickly developed other products to be used as substitutes for CFCs. Soon thereafter, the ozone layer began to heal.

Dealing with climate change is much more difficult than ozone depletion. CFCs had somewhat limited use, and alternatives were quickly discovered. In contrast, fossil fuel use is much more central to the world's economy, and its use is widespread throughout the world and through a variety of products. Efforts to achieve the objective of reduced GHG emissions, however, must continue. A critical step in this process is overcoming the political stalemate and getting everyone on board regarding the severity of the climate change problem. We need to understand that if we do not address climate issues, the consequences will be catastrophic.

The climate denial campaign has succeeded in the sense that many rural residents are unsure of the reality of climate change, and many of those who believe climate change is real do not consider it to be a high priority. Additionally, many have been convinced that policies to address climate change will be harmful to the economy. In fact, persons involved in the goods producing industries may pay the greatest costs if climate change is not addressed. Increases in the number and severity of forest fires will harm loggers. Farmers and ranchers will be harmed by longer and more severe droughts. Fishermen will be harmed by the changing acidity of the oceans.

A crucial step in addressing climate change is to find ways to avoid making a small segment of the population bare an inequitable share of the costs. Current discussions about climate policy place emphasis on reducing fossil fuel consumption (especially coal). This emphasis immediately puts persons and communities economically dependent on the fossil fuel industries on the defensive, as reducing GHG emissions puts their jobs in danger of being eliminated (as discussed in chapter 3). Thus, everyone benefits from policies that address climate change, but a small segment of the population pays most of the costs. Approaches to share the costs more equitably are essential. A part of this sharing may be a plan to retrain workers and develop employment opportunities for persons working in industries made obsolete by needed climate change policies. These types of ideas for changing economies will be a topic of chapter 10.

A critical part of efforts to address climate change is to rebuild the confidence of the general public in science. Providing people with a better understanding of how science works, the questions science can and cannot ask, and how the scientific process addresses relevant questions will be paramount. Achieving this goal must be the target of much thought and research.

## Western Rangelands, Sage Grouse Policy, and Rural Economic Development

Driving across much of the semiarid West, one can go mile after seemingly endless mile with little to see but scrubby, gray sagebrush. From the outset, settlers did not see much value in these sagebrush-covered lands, and extensive efforts were made to convert them to something perceived as more productive or valuable. Generally, the first choice was to bring irrigation water to make crop production possible. Large amounts of money, time, and labor were devoted to building dams to catch spring runoff and canals to carry water for many miles to parched lands. Through this process, thousands of acres of what were once sagebrush-covered rangelands were converted to productive farmland.

On the millions of acres impossible to irrigate, livestock grazing was typically the next choice. Beginning in about 1850 people began bringing cattle onto western rangelands, and it became widely accepted that livestock grazing was the most productive use of much western rangeland. Livestock numbers greatly expanded after the Civil War, and soon millions of cattle and sheep were grazing on western rangelands. Eventually livestock numbers far exceeded grazing capacity. The result was severe overgrazing, and many areas in the West may never recover (Donahue 1999). To protect rangelands from further damage, federal land management agencies, specifically the US Forest Service and Bureau of Land Management (BLM), were created to manage the millions of acres of rangelands owned by the federal government. The agencies determined the number of livestock that could graze in different locations sustainably and the time of year that livestock were allowed to graze. Livestock owners were required to purchase a permit before sheep and cattle were permitted on federal lands.

In trying to achieve the dual goals of sustainable livestock grazing and creating economically viable rural communities, federal land managers worked closely with ranchers as they sought to make the land more productive for livestock grazing. Specifically, great efforts were made to destroy sagebrush in the hope that it would be replaced by grass. Approaches to eliminate sagebrush included poison, fire, and dragging a large chain between two tractors to break the sagebrush off at ground level or pull it up by the roots. The significance of livestock grazing for western rangeland can be shown by the fact that by the beginning of the twenty-first century, about 85 percent of federal land was grazed by domestic livestock, and the Forest Service and BLM combined administer grazing permits to about 30,000 users who cover about 21.6 million animal unit months (one animal grazing in an area for one month is one animal unit month) (AUMs; Gentner and Tanaka 2002).

In addition, great efforts were made to locate mineral and energy resources on western rangelands. The land was extensively disrupted where resources were found, and roads and power lines to reach the resource disrupted even more land. Invasive species and changing predator populations have further altered western rangelands. In recent years, amenities have played an increasing role in the western economy. With modern information and communication technology, growing numbers of people are able to live in high-amenity areas and still be connected to employers, clients, or suppliers. As a consequence, the numbers of homes and residents in areas that previously were thinly populated have increased greatly.

Of special significance are exurban developments (Travis 2007). Exurban developments are areas of low-density housing where individuals (who tend to be relatively wealthy) live on acreages that may range from five to fifteen acres. In the amenity-rich areas of the West, many exurbs are in more remote rural areas, often in places previously undisturbed (Jackson-Smith et al. 2006). R. Brown et al. (2005) report that areas of low-density, exurban development beyond the urban fringe occupy nearly fifteen times more area than higher-density urban development. Exurban development results in a maze of roads and power lines to reach the scattered homes that are often only periodically lived in. These actions greatly disrupt native habitat (Hansen et al. 2005).

The result of decades of these wide-ranging changes is that the sagebrush-covered rangelands of the West have been dramatically altered. Like all ecosystems, the sagebrush ecosystem supports a complex and interdependent web of life. Consequently, quite a few species most dependent on the sagebrush ecosystem have seen their number drop significantly. Perhaps most notable of these species is the Greater Sage Grouse.

## Greater Sage Grouse

The Greater Sage Grouse (*Centrocercus urophasianus*) has been dramatically impacted by changes in sagebrush ecosystems (figure 8.1). As was the case with the spotted owl, in many ways sage grouse has become an instrument in the battle over the definition and use of rangeland, and issues extend far beyond sage grouse protection. Greater sage grouse are the largest of the upland grouse species and are known as a "landscape-scale bird" because of their need for large expanses of land to provide the habitat necessary for survival during various stages of their life. A population of smaller birds, Gunnison sage-grouse (*Centrocercus minimus*), has recently been recognized as a separate species. Gunnison sage-grouse are found in southwest Colorado and southeast Utah. On January 11, 2013, the US Fish and Wildlife Service (FWS) proposed to protect the Gunnison sage-grouse as an Endangered Species under the ESA.

Of special significance for sage grouse is the need for large, intact sagebrush habitat surrounding "leks." Leks are areas where male sage grouse concentrate during spring to perform their elaborate courtship rituals. During these rituals, males perform a strutting display and females observe the display and then mate with the one they consider to be the most attractive male. Nesting then occurs nearby, and it is essential that the habitat provides necessary

**FIGURE 8.1.** Greater sage-grouse (istockphoto.com)

cover for protection from predators and food for mothers and newly hatched young. Prime habitat includes large sagebrush mixed with certain grasses and forbs (Connelly et al. 2000; Hagen et al. 2007; Holloran and Anderson 2005). Sage grouse feed mainly on sagebrush during the winter, but also eat various other plants and insects during the rest of the year, and the presence of these plants and insects is especially critical during the nesting stage.

Not only do sage grouse require large amounts of intact sagebrush habitat, but also they are extremely loyal to their home. Both males and females typically return to the same lek each spring throughout their life. When the population is vibrant, a number of leks may be located near one another, and lek exchanges could occur with neighboring sage grouse populations that enhance genetic diversity. Severe problems occur if local populations become small and isolated, and it is most difficult to restore sage grouse to an area where they have been lost.

In recent decades, sage grouse numbers have dropped precipitously (Schroeder et al. 1999; Stiver et al. 2006). Estimates are that population numbers have declined from about 16 million to around 200,000. Sage grouse were once found throughout the intermountain West and into southern Canada, but they have been totally eliminated from more than half of their historical range (Naugle 2011; Schroeder et al. 2004). Depending on local conditions, grouse populations around some leks are doing very well, while others are struggling and still others have completely disappeared. With shrinking habitat, many sage grouse populations are now totally isolated from other sage grouse populations. Of areas where populations of sage grouse remain, more than half are on federal land, while significant portions (about one-third) are on privately owned land.

There is uncertainty about sage grouse numbers at the time of initial settlement by people of European descent. Numbers in the nineteenth century may have been much lower than during the early decades of the twentieth century. Sage grouse populations may have increased significantly after initial settlement as a result of expansion of sagebrush habitat resulting from overgrazing that caused some grasslands to be transformed into land covered by sagebrush. Suppression of predators may also have led to population increases. Population numbers likely peaked between 1920 and 1960. Since then, population numbers have steadily declined. A number of factors are believed to have led to recent drastic population declines:

1. Habitat loss from urban expansion. Wherever farming, ranching, mining, or amenity developments have occurred, communities have emerged with their homes, roads, businesses, and schools. The expansion of urban and exurban areas has significantly reduced areas of uninterrupted sagebrush habitat required by sage grouse. Western populations have grown very rapidly in recent decades, far exceeding population growth rates in other parts of the country, expansion that has exacerbated the loss of sagebrush ecosystems.

2. Invasive species. Often invasive species have significant negative consequences for native plants and animals, and they have had an impact on declining sage grouse populations. Consider, for example, the case of cheatgrass. Cheatgrass was inadvertently imported with wheat or other grains from the trans-Caspian steppes during the 1890s or early 1900s. Cheatgrass does very well in the intermountain West and expanded extremely rapidly, especially as overgrazing weakened native plants. Cheatgrass now dominates millions of acres, especially in the Great Basin, and its coverage is continually expanding (Pellant 1996). Cheatgrass does well because it

produces a large number of seeds; it effectively adapts to drought or other environmental conditions and, perhaps most important, has changed the fire ecology of areas where it grows. Cheatgrass grows quickly in spring and then dries much earlier in summer than other grasses. As a result, it is palatable for both livestock and wildlife for only a very short period of time. Then, because it dries early, cheatgrass becomes tinder that burns quickly and easily. Before the cheatgrass infestation, it is estimated that areas in the intermountain West would experience wildfire only once every thirty to seventy years; cheatgrass-infested areas now experience wildfires between every one and five years. Such high fire frequencies make survival most difficult for many native plant species, leaving the area even more susceptible to increased domination by cheatgrass that, in turn, does respond quickly and efficiently to fire. Thus, cheatgrass has replaced plants more palatable to the sage grouse diet and has resulted in a much higher frequency of fires, upsetting the habitat on which the grouse depends.

3. Energy development. The West has been the center of extensive energy development in recent years, and much of this development has occurred in areas that provide prime Sage Grouse habitat (Connelly et al. 2004; Naugle 2011). For example, Stoellinger (2014) notes that Wyoming is the state with the largest remaining sage grouse population and is the second leading state in the nation in total energy production. As of 2012, 81.7 percent of total natural gas produced and 86.6 percent of total coal produced in Wyoming were located on sage grouse range. In reviewing the literature on the implications of energy development for sage grouse populations, David Naugle (2011) reported that every study found that energy development hurt sage grouse populations. Roads to areas of energy development disrupt habitat, and the development itself could be very disruptive to the birds' local populations.

4. Predators. Changes in the numbers of predators that directly prey on sage grouse obviously impacts the birds' populations. The relationship, however, is complex. Of special significance, the elimination or extensive reduction of mesopredators (such as wolves, bears, and mountain lions) has resulted in increased numbers of the next level down of predators (e.g., coyotes and foxes; Prugh et al. 2009; Sergio et al. 2005; Sergio et al. 2008). Increased numbers of these smaller predators are a greater concern for sage grouse than are mesopredators; smaller predators are much more likely to target sage grouse, whereas mesopredators generally target larger prey.

5. Agriculture and livestock grazing. No question, expansion of cropland and extensive cultivation reduces sage grouse habitat. The focus of environmental and other groups, however, has been on reducing or eliminating livestock grazing from public lands to preserve sage grouse populations (Clifford 2002). Research on livestock grazing indicates that it is relatively low on the list of factors with negative implications for sage grouse populations. In fact, livestock grazing can have outcomes that are either positive or negative for the grouse depending on the timing and intensity of grazing (Beck and Mitchell 2000; Crawford et al. 2004). Grazing under certain circumstances can promote forb production that benefits these birds. Also, grazing has been found to be one of the more effective means of controlling invasive species such as cheatgrass. Typically, the negative consequences resulting from livestock grazing are from the herbicides that are used to eliminate sagebrush and thus encourage improved production of grass.

Another factor to consider in elimination of livestock grazing is the effect that the loss of grazing will have on the survival of ranches. Studies indicate (Tanaka et al. 2014; Torell et al. 2002) that reduced livestock grazing on public lands could have a significant negative impact on the economic survival of many farm/ranch operations. The general pattern is for the floundering operation to go out of business. Hannah Gosnell and W. R. Travis (2005) found that when ranches were sold in the post-1990 era, a majority were purchased by amenity and out-of-state buyers, and much of the land was subdivided into plots often used in exurban developments. Consequently, what was once open rangeland became disrupted. Since one-third of critical sage grouse habitat is privately owned land, the replacement of open ranchland with exurban development is likely to adversely affect sage grouse populations.

The concern of many in the West is that the sage grouse will be declared endangered under the ESA and that this declaration would then have severe negative economic implications as occurred with the spotted owl. Two questions about and endangered species classification are paramount:

1. Is declaring sage grouse endangered the best way to assure the birds' prosperity and survival? In 2010, the US Fish and Wildlife Service (FWS) concluded that rapidly declining numbers meant that the greater sage-grouse warranted federal protection under the ESA. A final decision about an ESA

listing would be made before September 30, 2015. While ESA listing could likely reduce habitat loss from urban / exurban expansion and energy development, it would do nothing about invasive species and predator problems. Also, there is concern that a "one-size fits all" policy would not be effective in the diverse West.

The residents of the West chose to seek to avoid an Endangered Species classification by implementing plans that would assure survival of the sage grouse in a way that would make the classification unnecessary. A critical aspect of this plan was the development of local working groups (LWGs). Soon, over sixty such partnership groups were organized to develop and implement local sage grouse management plans (Belton and Jackson-Smith 2010). Support from state governments and federal land management agencies (BLM and USFS) was evident from the beginning. Involvement from major environmental groups, the energy industry, and the agriculture industry was also critical. These LWGs are in accordance with an FWS regulation known as Section 4(d). Section 4(d) of the ESA provides the FWS with the ability to craft specific rules to protect a species. It requires an all-hands-on-deck approach and collaboration between federal, states, private, and industry stakeholders (Stoellinger 2014). Resulting from these cooperative efforts, plans were developed and implemented.

As an indication of the success of local efforts to preserve sage grouse habitat and thus its populations, the US Fish and Wildlife Service (FWS) announced on September 22, 2015, that the bird would not be ESA listed. The FWS maintained that the cooperation by individuals and organizations at the local level had created circumstances that had allowed the grouse to survive and thrive. All parties had worked together to manage land in a manner to preserve vital sage grouse habitat, and the results had been positive. Obviously, the goal is to continue efforts that help maintain sage grouse populations. Should their numbers begin to decline again, an Endangered Species listing is always an option.

2. The second question concerns the impacts of sage grouse policies on the economy of the West. Specifically, there was widespread consternation that Endangered Species listing would have significant negative implications for the energy and agriculture industries and therefore the economy of local communities. Some observers have speculated that negative outcomes associated with listing the Sage Grouse are so great that the listing would

not occur for political reasons. It should be remembered that economic impact is not a factor considered in a listing decision. Anyone doubting the US Fish and Wildlife Service's backbone to make unpopular decisions with huge economic repercussions should remember what happened with the spotted owl (Stoellinger 2014). So far, the approach of creating LWGs, which allow energy and agricultural industries to continue while main-taining the viability of sage grouse populations, appears to be working. I strongly maintain that the best approach for addressing nearly all problems is to have all parties sit around the same table, seek to thoroughly under-stand the issue, and then find compromise policies that best meet the needs of everyone concerned. This would include survival of the sage grouse (or any other species) and retention of jobs in the goods producing industries to help retain the viability of rural communities. Such actions could allow the survival of agriculture and energy industries in local areas that would allow them to be a part of a diversified economy.

## Relevance of Federal Regulations

The question asked at the beginning of this chapter is the extent to which regulations are necessary. No question industries could be more profitable if they weren't required to be concerned about air and water pollution. There are, however, "externalities." An externality is a cost or benefit resulting from an activity that affects an otherwise-uninvolved party who did not choose to incur that cost or benefit. For example, if I build a factory on a stream and release factory wastes into the stream, this action will have negative impli-cations for people downstream who use the stream in any way. If a factory pumps pollution into the air, factory owners benefit while everyone breath-ing polluted air pay the costs. The operators of many early mines made a great fortune. Those of us living today are paying the costs of cleanup. Little question that those benefitting from a product should pay the cost of produc-ing that product, even if this means that their profits decline or the cost of the product for the consumer increases.

Often persons paying the costs are those living in the future. You and I are paying the costs from the pollution resulting from mining endeavors in the past. With climate change, those of us living now receive the many comforts and advantages from the energy produced by fossil fuels. Most of us will not have to personally find a way to cope with vastly higher sea levels. Rather, we will pass these and other costs on to our children and grandchildren. Such behavior is both selfish and unfair.

A common way of controlling externalities is government control. For example, the air and water pollution control acts mentioned earlier were intended to make polluters pay the costs, rather than passing them on to those of us who breath the air or use the water. Centuries of experience have taught us policies to prevent some individuals from acting in a way that provides benefits to them while passing on the costs to others is the only way of preventing such actions. Sustainable and healthy communities not only require good jobs, but also a safe and clean environment. The level and type of regulations should be the product of ongoing debate. Clearly there is a fine line between protecting the environment and protecting jobs.

# 9

# Federal Land Management and Rural Economic Development

Federal land in the western United States is ubiquitous. Nearly 90 percent of the land in the state of Nevada is federally owned, as are about two-thirds of Utah and Idaho and more than one-half of Arizona, Oregon, and Wyoming. In California, the nation's most populous state, 46.9 percent of the land is federally owned. In total, nearly 1 million square miles (55.4 percent) of the land in the thirteen western states is owned and managed by the federal government. In comparison, in the thirty-seven nonwestern states less than 5 percent of the land is federally owned. Ninety percent of the federally owned land in the United States is in the West (Albrecht 2014a).

The implications are extensive. Federal land is effectively off limits for homes, farms, and businesses and is exempt from property tax. Such limitations most certainly provide some constraints to demographic and economic growth. Yet, on the other hand, federal land has historically provided grazing for thousands of cattle and sheep. Extensive amounts of timber have been harvested and minerals extracted from federal land. For decades, these resource-based industries were the economic backbone of many rural communities

DOI: 10.7330/9781607329510.c009

in the west (Frentz et al. 2004; Lorah and Southwick 2003). Wages paid to employees of the federal land management agencies represents a significant economic infusion to western communities. Additionally, by limiting development, federal land now provides open space and accessible amenities that make nearby communities more attractive to potential migrants and that draw millions of tourists each year (Albrecht 2004; Beyers and Nelson 2000; Hansen et al. 2002; Hunter et al. 2005; McGranahan 1999; Rasker and Hansen 2000; Rudzitis 1999; Saint Onge et al. 2007; Shumway and Davis 1996; Vias and Carruthers 2005).

From the beginning, federal land management has been fraught with controversy and has major implications on the economic viability of nearby rural communities. The explosiveness and emotional intensity of federal land management issues were again apparent during recent disputes at the Bundy Ranch in southeast Nevada, the Malheur National Wildlife Refuge in Oregon, and Grand Staircase Escalante and Bears Ears National Monuments in Utah, which will be discussed later in this chapter. While dramatic, these flare-ups are not terribly surprising and are part of an ongoing controversy that in recent years has resulted in death threats to federal rangers and in high-ranking BLM officials feeling it necessary to be accompanied by security when traveling in parts of the West. Through the years, many have argued that the nation would be better served if federal lands were either privatized or returned to management by the states (Cawley 1993; Culhane 2013; Nelson 1995). This chapter explores the source of these concerns and approaches to address them.

## Emergence of Federal Land

At the close of the American Revolution, the original boundaries of the United States included all land east of the Mississippi River, south of the Great Lakes and north of the thirty-first parallel (the present northern boundary of Florida). The land west of the present boundaries of the original thirteen states were claimed by Massachusetts, Connecticut, New York, Virginia, North Carolina, South Carolina, and Georgia. The six states that did not have western claims demanded that the other states cede their claims to the federal government. These cessions gave 1.48 million square miles to the public domain of the United States. As the young country grew through purchases (such as the Louisiana Purchase from France or Alaska from Russia) or conquest (such as the Mexican-American War of 1848), the newly acquired land became a part of the public domain and was managed by the federal government (Nelson 1995).

For the first century of our nation's existence, federal ownership was perceived as merely temporary, and the prevailing US policy was to get land into the hands of private settlers for the purpose of developing the country. The best known of the federal land disposal policies was the Homestead Act of 1862. After laying claim to 160 acres and paying a small registration fee, an individual could gain clear ownership of this land after five years by living on the land and making improvements. Through this and other homestead laws, over 1.78 million square miles of land were claimed by individuals and families and resulted in farms and communities being established throughout the country. The availability of this land was the magnet that drew millions of settlers to this country from Europe. Through homestead laws and other policies, the vast majority of land east of the Rocky Mountains was in private ownership by the end of the nineteenth century.

Vast tracts of western land, however, were unclaimed by homesteaders and thus remained in federal ownership. During the nineteenth century, settlers continually moved westward, seeking areas where traditional natural resources allowed them to earn an economic livelihood. Areas with the greatest concentration of relevant resources were in highest demand because these areas could support the largest populations and life could be lived more abundantly. Development in much of the West, however, was greatly stymied by the relative lack of these traditional natural resources. Much of the West consists of towering mountains, deep canyons, and vast nearly waterless deserts. Such landscapes are not conducive to agriculture and often lack other economically important resources. Thus, in many parts of the West it was virtually impossible to make a living on the 160 acres available to homesteaders. Unclaimed western lands that remained in federal ownership ranged from the spectacular (such as areas that became Grand Canyon or Grand Tetons National Parks) to the barren, flat, and generally unappealing. What all of this unclaimed land had in common, however, was a lack of the traditional resources that would allow individuals, families, or businesses an opportunity to earn a living (Albrecht 2014a; Jakus 2016).

When continued federal efforts, such as the "Enlarged Homestead Act" of 1909 (which allowed settlers to claim 320 acres) and the "Stock-Raising Homestead Act" of 1916 (which allowed settlers to claim 640 acres), failed to induce settlers to move to the arid, semiarid, and mountainous regions of the West, it became apparent that the role of the federal government in land management would of necessity become more permanent and involved. In 1872, Congress made its first important reservation of public land by creating Yellowstone National Park. Just less than 3,500 square miles (more than 2.2 million acres) of federal land were withdrawn from settlement and sale and dedicated as a public park "for the pleasure and recreation of the people." Within a few decades, other areas such as Sequoia and Yosemite were also preserved as National Parks.

A growing awareness of the need for conservation resulted from concerns that federal lands were being exploited. In the late nineteenth century, federal lands were being used by individuals and companies for the indiscriminate harvesting of timber, the widespread and unrestrained grazing of cattle and sheep, and the uncontrolled removal of minerals, all for private use and gain. In many respects, federal lands represented a vast "Tragedy of the Commons" (Hardin 1968). Thus, calls for the more effective management of federal lands grew more persistent. As a consequence, during the early decades of the twentieth century, four major agencies (the US Forest Service, National Park Service, Bureau of Land Management and US Fish and Wildlife Service) were created to manage federal lands (Albrecht 2014a). Each of these agencies manages different types of lands, and they have varying management goals and objectives (Davis 2001; Fortmann and Fairfax 1991; Hays 2009; Merrill 2002; Nie 2008; Robinson 1975). Generally, the federal land management agencies were created with the support and encouragement of state and local governments (Libecap 1993).

In general, most Park Service lands are managed for resource preservation, and consequently grazing, mining, lumbering or other activities that would support resource-based industries are forbidden. In contrast, most US Forest Service and Bureau of Land Management lands are managed for multiple use, and resource extraction industries have traditionally been allowed. The US Fish and Wildlife Service manage lands that are a part of the National Wildlife Refuge System. These lands are very diverse, and uses vary by the unique goals of each refuge. The vast majority of lands in the National Wildlife Refuge system are in Alaska.

Considering the Wilderness Preservation System is also important. Following the Wilderness Preservation Act of 1964, Congress has set aside some land managed by each of the four major land management agencies as Wilderness. The Wilderness Act defines Wilderness as land

> where the earth and its community of life are untrammeled by man, where man himself is a visitor who does not remain . . . generally appears to have been affected primarily by the forces of nature, with the imprint of man's work substantially unnoticeable . . . has outstanding opportunities for solitude or a primitive and unconfined type of recreation.

Consequently, extractive activities are generally prohibited on Wilderness land.

## Concerns with Federal Land Management

For generations, many individuals, families and communities in the rural West have been economically dependent on public lands. For many farmers and ranchers, the opportunity to have livestock graze on federal land was a vital part of their agricultural enterprise. Many loggers made a living by cutting trees and miners by extracting minerals from federal lands. With their economic survival dependent on supportive public land policies, people created a variety of interest groups that have then extended great effort to influence the policy agenda of federal land management agencies. For decades, loggers, miners, and ranchers significantly influenced the policy agenda of the Forest Service and BLM. Policies that adversely impacted these user groups were met with strong resistance (Culhane 2013). Largely, western delegations to Congress supported interest groups desiring policies that allowed continued grazing, logging, mining, and other uses of federal land that provided economic opportunities for individuals and communities. For nonwestern representatives, the issues were not high enough on their priority list to provide significant objections.

Beginning in the 1960s, other individuals and interest groups with very different goals gained enough power to alter the federal land management policy agenda. Riding on public support generated by the environmental movement, environmental groups sought to preserve some public lands for amenity, aesthetic, or recreational uses and to limit or eliminate grazing, logging, mining, and other extractive uses. Support for these groups increased as the proportion of US residents living in urban communities increased. Many urban people were not directly dependent on federal lands to make a living and were thus more interested in amenity and other uses of this land. Many urban and nonwestern residents argued that public lands belonged to all Americans and were opposed to these lands serving primarily as an economic asset to a small number of loggers and ranchers. Improved transportation and growing wealth further resulted in more Americans visiting public lands and forming strong attachments with specific places (Eisenhauer et al. 2000).

This growing public interest and support prompted involvement in federal land issues by elected officials from throughout the nation. Resistance began to grow to the traditional western policy agenda. Continued extractive uses of federal lands have met with additional challenges from scientifically based ecological studies that have found that some traditional uses of resources were causing detrimental and sometimes irreparable damage to the environment and even to public health (Anderson et al. 2008).

The implications of these policies were substantial. As noted in chapter 8, a number of decisions forever changed federal land management policies, and logging and mining on federal land declined sharply. Similarly, livestock grazing on BLM land decreased from 18.2 million AUMs (animal unit months) in 1954 to 7.9 million AUMs in 2013. With passage of these laws and subsequent declines in opportunities to use federal lands for economic gain, ranchers, loggers, miners and other users of western public lands, small-town residents, and their interest groups responded strongly. The culmination of these efforts became known as the "Sagebrush Rebellion."

*The Sagebrush Rebellion*

In 1979, the Nevada legislature took the first shot in the Sagebrush Rebellion by enacting a law claiming title to all BLM land within the state's boundaries. Other western states followed suit with similar legislation. The Sagebrush Rebellion was simply a protest against increasing environmental regulations and a concern that the enactment of these policies would greatly hinder opportunities to make a living in the goods producing industries by residents of the rural West (Cawley 1993).

Major alternatives to federal management suggested by the Sagebrush Rebellion's supporters included privatization and having primary management authority of federal land revert to the states. As the movement progressed, many adherents expressed opposition to large-scale privatization because of fears of who could and would buy federal land and what they would do with it. A real fear for western public land users is that wealthy individuals and groups with environmental leanings would buy vast amounts of federal land and turn it into an untouchable wilderness preserve or a playground only accessible to the wealthy. Thus, state control became the primary option of choice. Supporters maintained that states would manage the lands sustainably but in a manner consistent with western values; continued logging, grazing, and mining on some land would provide jobs and help maintain the economic viability of rural communities. Bills were introduced in Congress in Washington, DC, to give western states control and management of federal lands in the west. These bills, however, died in committee.

In the years since the birth of the Sagebrush Rebellion, little or no headway has been made in having federal ownership revert to the states. The ideas, however, have not been forgotten and have again become a significant political topic in recent years. In 2013, Utah H.B. 142 required an economic analysis of the implications of transferring land management responsibility from the federal government to the state of Utah. Utah H.B. 148 then sought to transfer title of 31.2 million acres of federal land to the state of Utah. The analysis required by H.B. 142 found that the state benefitted from $150 million in federal payroll to land management employees and that the federal government paid $248 million in land management costs. If title were transferred to the state, these assets would have to be managed by the state. The only way such a transfer would make economic sense for the state is if the state could generate sufficient revenue from this land, primarily by resource development, to offset the costs. The economic analysis prepared by economists from University of Utah, Utah State University, and Weber State University found that only under certain scenarios and circumstances would the transfer make sense economically for the state. State ownership would be economically problematic when energy prices were low or when costly wildfires occurred (Jakus et al. 2017).

Additionally, a number of studies have examined the relationship between the proportion of land in a county that is federally owned and demographic and economic change within that county. These studies have consistently found that the presence of federal land, in general, and protected land, in particular, are positively related to population and economic growth (Duffy-Deno 1998; Frentz et al. 2004; Holmes and Hecox 2004). Protected lands include National Parks, National Monuments, Wilderness, and other federal lands where traditional extractive resource uses are explicitly excluded. Thus, contrary to the arguments of many western residents, higher levels of federal land, especially protected federal land, results in higher rather than lower levels of economic and demographic growth. Figures 9.1 and 9.2, for example, show that counties with higher proportions of federal lands and more protected lands had higher rates of population growth from 1930 to 2010. Rather than being an economic drag, the presence of federal land in a county actually seems to be an economic engine and has been for decades.

That federal land should act as an economic engine makes some sense when it provided timber and grazing to nearby residents. Yet, even as traditional resource uses of federal lands (logging, grazing, mining, etc.) have declined, economic and demographic growth in lands with extensive federal lands has accelerated. Because the demographic and economic significance of these resource-based industries has declined, the primary employer of Americans, even in rural communities, is now the service sector, with employment in the resource industries becoming an increasingly small proportion of total employment. At the present time, the variable with the strongest relationship to economic and demographic growth is amenities rather than board feet harvested or grazing AUMs (Albrecht 2004).

In recent decades, people with creative class or geographically mobile jobs or individuals with investment or retirement income often move to high-amenity communities to enhance their quality of life. Today, fewer jobs require the presence of traditional resources, and more people have freedom to live where they desire. When people have greater freedom to choose where they will live, many will choose select, high-amenity communities (Albrecht 2004; Beyers and Nelson 2000; Boyle and Halfacree 1998; Cromartie and Wardwell 1999; Green 2001; Henderson and McDaniel 1998; McGranahan 1999, 2009; McGranahan and Wojan 2007; Nord and Cromartie 1997; Otterstrom and Shumway 2003; Rudzitis 1999; Rudzitis and Johansen 1991; Saint Onge et al. 2007; Shumway and Davis 1996; Shumway and Otterstrom 2001). In such an environment, it may make more sense economically to preserve land for amenities rather than to push for more logging, grazing, mining, and other extractive resource uses. This concept is discussed in more detail in chapter 10.

To better understand the issues associated with federal land management policies, two western communities are discussed.

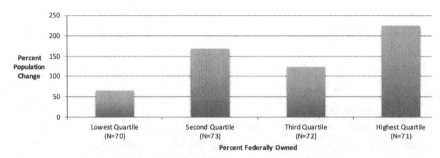

**FIGURE 9.1.** Relationship between percent of land federally owned and population change in western nonmetro counties, 1930–2010

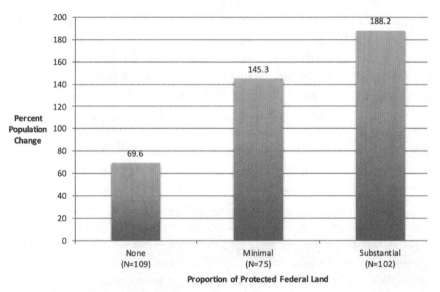

**FIGURE 9.2.** Relationship between proportion of protected federal land and population change in western nonmetro counties, 1930–2010

*Bunkerville, Nevada*

Bunkerville is located in Clark County, Nevada, about ninety miles northeast of Las Vegas. This desert region has blistering hot summers and very little precipitation. According to the 2010 Census, the community's population was 1,303. For the time being, the town's most famous resident is Cliven

Bundy. The Bundy family purchased farmland near Bunkerville in 1948. Like thousands of farm/ranch operations throughout the West, the Bundy Ranch consists of privately owned and irrigated farmland to produce crops to feed livestock during winter months. The operation also consists of grazing permits to allow livestock to graze on nearby federal land (in this case managed by the BLM) during other parts of the year. Prior to 1993, Bundy, like thousands of other ranchers throughout the West, paid for his federal grazing permits. Then, in 1993, some federal land was excluded from livestock grazing to protect the desert tortoise, which had recently been declared endangered under the Endangered Species Act. From this point on, Bundy refused to make further payments. He argued that his family has been raising cattle on the land since 1877 and so his rights to the land supersede those of the BLM, a federal agency that didn't exist in 1877. He also asserts that the state of Nevada, rather than the federal government, really owns the land. In fact, he doesn't recognize the legal existence of the United States.

Because of Bundy's failure to make lease payments, the BLM used a series of court cases and legal actions to prevent him from grazing his livestock on federal land. Bundy, however, simply ignored these legal injunctions and continued to graze his cattle on BLM land. Eventually, the amount of money owed by Bundy to the federal government was in excess of $1 million (Neiwert 2017). Finally, in March 2014, 145,604 acres of federal land in Clark County were temporarily closed for the "capture, impound, and removal of trespass cattle." A roundup of cattle by federal agents began on April 5, with the goal of selling the cattle to partially pay Bundy's debt. Within a few days, about 400 of Bundy's cattle had been gathered and penned. However, efforts to continue the roundup were then met by a group of armed protesters who gathered at the Bundy Ranch. The protestors included militia member and others opposed to the actions of the BLM. On a couple of occasions, there were tense armed standoffs with heavily armed federal agents and Clark County Deputy sheriffs facing off against heavily armed protesters. Finally, the Clark County sheriff and BLM director negotiated with Bundy to release the cattle in order to deescalate the situation.

Similar events have occurred in other parts of the West. On January 2, 2016, a group of armed protesters led by Ammon Bundy (Cliven's son) took over the Malheur National Wildlife Refuge near Burns, Oregon, in Harney County. The protesters initially objected to the imprisonment of local ranchers

Dwight Hammond Jr. and his son Steven Hammond. The Hammonds had been convicted of arson on federal land. After occupying the refuge, Ammon Bundy announced that the occupiers wouldn't leave until local property owners had been given control of refuge land. On January 26, Oregon State Police and the FBI confronted protest leaders as they were traveling to a community meeting. During the confrontation, one of the protesters, Robert "LaVoy" Finicum, was shot and killed and five people arrested, including Ammon Bundy. Later that day, six more protesters were arrested. The final occupiers didn't leave the refuge until February 10. On that same day, Cliven Bundy was arrested at Portland International Airport. After long and complicated court hearings, the Bundys and their accomplices were acquitted on all charges showing the difficulty of finding a jury in the West who will convict persons for protesting how federal lands are used (Neiwert 2017).

The standoff between the Bundy families and others with the federal government continues. Some view the Bundys as heroes. They are often given standing ovations when they attend meetings in the West. Others maintain that Bundy is simply a welfare rancher living off of taxpayer subsidies, since he refuses to make his lease payments.

In continuing their protest about federal land management, another of Cliven Bundy's sons, Ryan Bundy, led a group of protestors driving all-terrain vehicles into Recapture Canyon in San Juan County, Utah. Recapture Canyon is an area that has been established as off limits to motorized vehicles in an effort to protect ancient American Indians archaeological sites. This protest received greater publicity because of the involvement of San Juan County (Utah) commissioner Phil Lyman. Bundy, Lyman, and other protesters argued that Recapture Canyon was a beautiful place, people had the right to see it, and the federal government didn't have the right to prevent people from seeing the canyon. The protesters were arrested, and during the trial, Lyman received a letter of support from Utah governor Gary Herbert and donations from individuals from around the West to offset Lyman's court costs. Lyman was sentenced to ten days in jail.

*National Monument Designation*

In September 1996 Democrat president Bill Clinton used the Antiquities Act to create the Grand Staircase Escalante National Monument (GSENM) in Southern Utah. With a stroke of his pen, the president set aside nearly 1.9 million acres (larger than the state of Delaware) as a National Monument. The dimensions of GSENM are roughly 100 miles by 200 miles. This federally owned land managed by the BLM had once been open to livestock grazing, mineral and energy extraction, and timber harvest. As a National Monument, the land would now be managed to preserve its natural beauty and historic artifacts. Extractive uses would be largely eliminated. The cattle that were grazing had to be removed, and a planned coal mine was nixed. Since the land had previously been managed by the BLM, the new National Monument would continue to be managed by the BLM. GSENM became the first National Monument ever to be managed by the BLM.

The stated purpose for preservation as a National Monument was to protect the unquestioned natural beauty and archaeological wonders within GSENM. Red rock cliffs, natural arches, and other geological wonders abound. Of special significance are sedimentary rock sequences shaped like a gigantic staircase that preserves more of earth's history than any other place on the planet. Additionally, many dinosaur fossils and early American Indian ruins have been discovered.

No question, political expediency was also a significant factor in GSENM preservation. The monument was created during the homestretch of the 1996 presidential campaign, and it helped Clinton's campaign secure support from environmental groups and environmentally conscience people throughout the country. Republican political leaders in Utah and many local residents, however, were furious. Clinton was willing to pay that price, as he was fully aware that he was going to lose the state of Utah anyway. Recognizing the feelings of Utah residents, Clinton choice to announce the creation of the National Monument at Grand Canyon National Park in Arizona, even though GSENM is completely within Utah.

The Antiquities Act, through which Clinton created GSENM, was passed by Congress and then signed into law by President Theodore Roosevelt in 1906. This controversial act gives the president power to create National Monuments on federal land by presidential proclamation. When originally passed, the stated purpose of the Antiquities Act was to allow the president to protect significant natural, cultural, or scientific features. Using this act, preservation of land as a National Monument is much quicker and easier than creation of a National Park, which requires passage by Congress.

Since becoming law, the Antiquities Act has been used more than 100 times, often with significant controversy (Squillace 2002). The Antiquities Act was used to create Grand Canyon and Grand Tetons as National Monuments at a time when there was insufficient congressional support for National Park designation. Both later became National Parks when the necessary political support was obtained. Several other National Monuments created by the Antiquities Act have later become National Parks, including Arches, Canyonlands, and Capitol Reef National Parks in Utah (Righter 1989). Many others remain National Monuments.

Some National Monuments created by the Antiquities Act are huge while others have been much less than one acre. For example, the Father Millet Cross National Monument is only 30 meters squared. At the other extreme, in 1978, President Jimmy Carter used the Antiquities Act to withdraw 56 million acres from the public domain in Alaska (Johannsen 1980). With this land safely preserved as National Monuments, he was then able to use this as political leverage to help assure passage of the Alaska National Interest Lands Conservation Act (ANILCA) of 1980. ANILCA protects over 100 million acres of federal land in Alaska, created 7 new National Parks (Gates of the Arctic; Glacier Bay; Katmai; Kenai Fjords; Kobuk Valley; Lake Clark; and Wrangell-St. Elias) and expanded the size of Denali National Park. President Carter had preserved much of the land in these National Parks as National Monuments through use of the Antiquities Act two years earlier. ANILCA doubled the size of the National Park System and tripled the amount of land designated as Wilderness. The act also allocated vast amounts of land as part of the National Wildlife Refuge System.

For the president to have so much power has always been extremely controversial. Several times, the President's use of the Antiquities Act has been taken to court and on occasions reached the Supreme Court. In each case the court ruled that the Act is constitutional (Squillace 2002).

In the case of GSENM, opposition from the Utah congressional delegation and some local residents was based on concern that National Monument preservation would have negative economic implications for local communities in the form of lost grazing, logging, and mining opportunities. Persons supporting GSENM creation maintained that the loss of grazing and mining revenue would be more than offset by increased tourism. One way to better understand the socioeconomic consequences of GSENM for local communities is to explore what actually happened in communities bordering on the National Monument that were impacted by National Monument designation. To accomplish this goal, an examination of the Southern Utah communities of Escalante and Boulder is provided.


*Escalante and Boulder, Utah*

The communities of Escalante and Boulder, Utah, are located in Garfield County in Southern Utah and both are near the borders of GSENM. Mormon settlers established these communities in the late 1800s. From the outset, these communities were economically dependent on irrigated agriculture supported by livestock grazing on surrounding public lands. Much of the land where livestock grazing historically occurred is now within the National Monument.

Initially, the geographic isolation of Escalante and Boulder was extreme. Not only was the distance to urban areas substantial, but also existing roads through the rugged mountains and canyons of Southern Utah were treacherous. Escalante is sixty-six winding miles east of the Garfield County seat of Panguitch on State Highway 12. The road from Panguitch to Escalante goes near the entrance of Bryce Canyon National Park. Continuing east from Escalante, it is another twenty-seven miles to Boulder. Until recently, the road connecting Boulder and Escalante was often nearly impassible, especially a section that is now within GSENM known as "Hells Backbone." As a child, I remember riding in the front seat of the family pickup with my Dad as we drove over Hells Backbone. The road was barely wide enough for a single vehicle, and there was a sharp drop-off of several hundred feet on both sides of the road. I was terrified. The kids from Boulder had to cross this road twice each day going back and forth from school in Escalante. As a measure of isolation, Boulder did not have regular mail or telephone service until the 1960s.

From Boulder, Highway 12 then turns north and crosses Boulder Mountain before reaching the small communities of Wayne County. The distance from Boulder to Torrey on the edge of Capitol Reef National Park in Wayne County is about forty miles. Until recently, to reach Wayne County from Escalante in the summer would require driving over Hells Backbone to Boulder and then over the mountain to Wayne County. During the winter, the

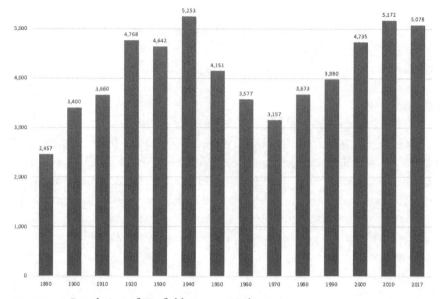

**FIGURE 9.3.** Population of Garfield County, Utah, 1890–2017

road over Boulder Mountain was closed because of deep snow. This meant a trip to Wayne County would require a detour that included a 66-mile drive to Panguitch and then another 100 miles from Panguitch to Wayne County.

Recently, the roads have been improved to some degree. Snow removal allows the road over Boulder Mountain to remain open during the winter. Also, the Hells Backbone section of Highway 12 has been widened and guardrails installed. In my opinion the road from Capitol Reef National Park in Wayne County, over Boulder Mountain, through GSENM and Bryce Canyon National Park to Panguitch is one of the most spectacular drives in America.

Both communities reached a population peak in 1940—Escalante with 1,161 residents and Boulder with 216. As with farm-dependent communities everywhere, the population plummeted during the middle decades of the twentieth century as farm technology improved and each farmer was able to operate a larger farm. By 1970, the population of Escalante was 638, while in Boulder the number of residents had been reduced to only 93. Figure 9.3 shows population trends in Garfield County, where both Escalante and Boulder are located. The county reached a population peak in 1940 with 5,253 residents. The population then declined sharply and in 1970 the county's population was 3,157.

Since 1970, the population of Escalante has increased slightly, while the number of residents in Boulder has more than doubled. Similarly, the population in Garfield County increased as well. In 2010, the population of Escalante was 797 and that of Boulder was 226. No question, some of this growth can be attributed to GSENM designation. Escalante and Boulder resemble high-amenity communities throughout the West that have experienced a reversal of population losses in recent decades, and noted previously, amenities and federal land ownership are related to demographic and economic growth. Modern technology has reduced costs associated with distance; the number of miles to Escalante and Boulder from elsewhere has not changed, but improved roads have made the drive easier. Additionally, better information and communication technology allows residents of places such as Boulder and Escalante to be in much closer contact with the larger world and with family and friends wherever they may be. Given greater freedom to live where they wish, many people chose to live in high-amenity rural communities. Also, the number of tourists passing through has skyrocketed, which has made it possible for some hotels, restaurants, and gas stations to open.

While tourism and the service sector have expanded, employment in resource-based industries continues to decline. Perhaps some of the resource jobs have been lost because of the National Monument designation. There is no question, however, that improving technology that allows machines to replace human labor in the production process has resulted in the loss of even more jobs. The extent to which job losses in the resource industries of Escalante and Boulder is a consequence of GSENM as opposed to being a part of continuing national trends toward reduced employment in resource-based industries is an important question for which we don't have an adequate answer. A careful study by Paul Jakus (2016) found that GSENM designation had economic impacts that were neither greatly positive nor greatly negative. Some sectors of the economy benefited; others did not.

With declines in resource-based employment, both Escalante and Boulder have become increasingly dependent on tourism and the service sector. Unfortunately, there are obvious problems associated with an economic dependence on tourism as described in chapter 7. Tourism in this area is seasonal; the vast majority of visitors come during the summer months of June, July, and August. Consequently, tourism-related businesses struggle during the off-season and many employees are simply laid off. Another problem is that wages tend to be very low in most tourist-related jobs. Waiting tables in restaurants and cleaning hotel rooms are jobs that have never paid high wages. Further, Escalante still lacks many of the comforts and entertainment opportunities that many tourists desire. Bryce Canyon National Park is only forty miles away and rather than stay in Escalante, many tourists simply make the drive and stay in the more established tourism community.

While some new residents have moved to Escalante and Boulder, most are retired persons seeking to take advantage of the exceptional amenities in the area. In most cases, these persons no longer have children at home. The other growing population segment includes persons working in the tourism sector. In most cases, these individuals are young, without families, and are only in town until their summer job ends. At the end of the summer, they either return to college or go elsewhere to find a job. Economically, there is no way to stay because tourism jobs in Escalante are seasonal and the pay is inadequate to make it a career or to support a family.

I have had personal experience with the lack of services in Escalante during the off-season. One year during February I drove to Escalante for a meeting with community leaders. When I arrived, only one, fast-food restaurant was open, and so I had dinner there. After the meeting, I stayed in a local hotel. In the morning when I awoke and was ready to drive home, there wasn't a single place open for breakfast. I bought a Diet Coke and a piece of beef jerky at the gas station and drove to another community to eat breakfast.

In the case of Escalante and Boulder, amenity-related growth has failed to attract families with children. When associated with the continuing decline of employment in the resource industries (that do tend to be family centered), the result has been a severe decline in student enrollment in Escalante schools. Figure 9.4 presents data showing changes in the total number of students enrolled in Escalante schools (K–12) from 2001 to 2015. The rapid downward trend is obvious. By 2015, the average grade had only eleven students. For some high school classes, the number of graduates is in single digits.

Operating schools this small presents serious problems. First, per-student costs are very high. In general, the number of students per teacher is less in small schools than in larger schools. Small rural schools also have other economy-of-scale problems. Many technologies or programs have a substantial initial cost, whether 10 students or 5,000 students use the technology or

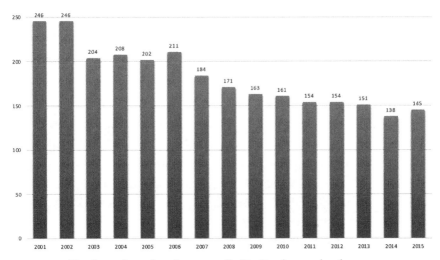

**FIGURE 9.4.** Total number of students enrolled in Escalante schools, 2001–2015

program. As a consequence, urban schools are advantaged because their cost per student is lower.

Second, in very small schools, it is very difficult to provide the range or quality of programs to help students succeed. For example, a small school can likely only afford one math or science teacher. Even in a best-case scenario, it is impossible for this one teacher to offer the range of classes and learning opportunities that a student will get in a large urban school, where there are multiple math or science teachers. Also troubling is the problem that emerges if the one teacher for a particular subject is not very good. In a large school, with multiple children to choose from, students can generally avoid the poor teacher and take necessary classes from someone more competent.

More fundamentally, the small rural school often has trouble attracting qualified teachers in the first place. In general, wages in rural schools tend to be lower. Further, most teachers prefer to be in an environment where they have colleagues. The problems of attracting qualified teachers are amplified in rural schools because when the schools do succeed in attracting a talented teacher, this teacher is often lost to an urban school after a few years. Meanwhile the schools are stuck with poor teachers because no one else wants them. I personally experienced these problems while enrolled in a small high school. The only math teacher in my high school happened to be a really bad teacher. My subsequent lack of math preparation haunted me throughout my college career. When our school was fortunate enough to have a really good basketball coach, this coach would last about two years until a larger school hired him away from us. Meanwhile our school would be stuck with the bad coaches until they were fired.

If the number of students in Escalante schools continues to decline, the Garfield County School District is faced with a difficult dilemma. Keeping the schools open as enrollment declines is problematic for the reasons described above. With distances so great, closing the schools and busing the kids to other schools are also not palatable options. For example, for kids living in Boulder the options are (1) 27 miles to Escalante and then another 40 miles to the Bryce Canyon schools, or (2) 40 miles over a mountain that often experiences severe winter weather to Wayne County schools.

In sum, in Escalante and Boulder the economic and social costs of GSENM creation may be substantial. Additional research to determine the extent to which this assessment is true, however, is greatly needed. Most significant, a decline in the number of jobs that pay a livable income has led to a reduction in the number of families with children. As a consequence, the survival of the communities as places to live and raise a family is very much in doubt.

What has happened in Escalante and Boulder seems in direct contrast to research findings described in the previous chapter. It was noted that a positive relationship has been found between amenities and federal land ownership with demographic and economic growth. The fact that Escalante and Boulder are different amplifies the problem of trying to generalize national findings to each specific situation. Every circumstance is different, and it is important to recognize individual differences. Their distinct situation also makes it apparent that outcomes are complex and that focusing on any single outcome may be problematic. For example, population growth did occur—this growth, however, did not extend to families and children. Additionally, perhaps the outcomes are a function of the small size and physical isolation of these communities. It may be possible that in larger and less-isolated communities, an action such as creation of GSENM would have led to demographic and economic growth. Another conclusion is that the creation of jobs in one sector doesn't provide much help for those employed in a different sector. For instance, construction of a new hotel is of little solace to a person who has lost their jobs as a miner or rancher. Obviously much more research is needed.

The majority of Garfield County residents have opposed the creation of GSENM. As a consequence, in the 2016 presidential election, Hillary Clinton received only 15 percent of Garfield County votes.

## Recent Developments in Federal Land Management

On December 28, 2016, President Barack Obama utilized the Antiquities Act to set aside 1.35 million acres in southeast Utah (all of it in San Juan County) as the Bears Ears National Monument. The process was very similar to what occurred twenty years earlier with the establishment of GSENM. Creation of Bears Ears National Monument was supported by local American Indian tribes and both local and national environmental groups. Many of these individuals and groups released statements of support. Some examples: Shawn Capoose, of the Ute Tribe, stated,

> President Obama has demonstrated today that our Native American heritage cannot be ignored. This national monument is the right solution at the right time, and we are pleased that the President has taken this step to ensure Bears Ears will remain in as pristine a condition as possible for generations to come. (Native News Online, December 31, 2016)

Scott Groene, executive director of Southern Utah Wilderness Alliance, stated:

> We applaud the President's decision and congratulate the Bears Ears Inter-Tribal Coalition for this historic protection of their ancestral homeland. The Monument will long benefit Utahans and Americans. It is the product of years of public discussion where all agreed this landscape is worthy of permanent protection. (*Salt Lake Tribune*, December 29, 2016)

On the other hand, local and state elected officials expressed dismay. The San Juan County Commission released the following statement:

> Today San Juan County mourns after President Barack Obama gave into pressure from extreme environmental groups, out-of-state tribal leaders,

and corporate interests by designating the 1.35 million-acre Bears Ears National Monument. The push for a monument did not originate from those most impacted by this decision; instead, it came from outside special interest groups who used deception and collusion to drown out local voices. San Juan County has only to look to our neighbors in Garfield and Kane counties to see the devastating consequences this process produces—the destruction of archaeological and cultural resources, the closure of public schools, and a shattered economy. Our families, our local tribes, and our community deserve better—they deserve to be heard and respected. As elected representatives of San Juan County, we call on Congress and the incoming president to heed the voices of locals who care for and love our county's public lands the most by rescinding this monument designation. (*KSL News*, December 28, 2016)

Utah congressional representative Chris Stewart stated,

The creation of the Bears Ears National Monument marks the second time in the recent past that a president has used the Antiquities Act to lock up millions of acres of land in Utah without daring to set foot in the state. I am disgusted by the process and will fight this monument with every tool at my disposal, including through the appropriations process. (*KSL News*, December 28, 2016)

The drama didn't end with the creation of Bears Ears National Monument. On December 4, 2017, President Trump traveled to Utah to announce that he was reducing the size of both Grand Staircase Escalante National Monument and Bears Ears National Monument. GSENM was reduced in size by about one-half, while Bears Ears was reduced by 85 percent. What remains of GSENM was divided into three sections that do not touch one another, while Bears Ears National Monument is divided into two unconnected sections. No doubt, this is not the end of the story. Before the ink was dry on the president's proclamation, several organizations had filed suit, arguing that this action was illegal. While the courts have previously ruled that the president doesn't have the right to eliminate a National Monument created by the Antiquities Act, the courts haven't ruled on whether the president has the power to reduce their size. There is also talk about Congress trying to pass a regulation that eliminates the Antiquities Act. Obviously, the end of this story is not yet written.

## Federal Regulations and Rural Economic Development

Initially, the Bundy protest received significant support from conservative talk show hosts and conservative politicians. Many backed off after gaining a better understanding of the issues and especially following racist comments by Bundy. The point for current discussion is that there was obviously considerable pent-up anger and frustration toward the federal government in general and federal land management agencies in particular that resulted in significant initial support for Bundy. Similarly, the reactions to National Monument designation are again evident of pent-up anger.

In chapters 8 and 9, examples were provided of circumstances in which some rural residents feel that federal policies and regulations have had negative implications for the economies of rural communities. Moving forward, my hope is that policy development in the future will consider a full range of consequences. The goods producing industries remain critical for the nation and can be a critical part of the economy of rural communities. That said, as noted again and again in this book, employment in these industries has been on the decline for decades, and this trend will continue. In most cases, communities with extensive federal land have the advantage of extensive amenities. Chapter 10 describes how communities can take advantage of amenities and federal land to develop a viable twenty-first century economy.

# 10

## Building a Twenty-First-Century Economy for Rural America

In the years to come, the world will still need the products made available by the goods producing industries. Food, energy, minerals, and timber remain essential parts of a twenty-first century economy. Manufacturing to transform raw materials into useful products remains critical. Employment in the goods producing industries can, and if possible, should, continue to be an important part of a community's economy. As apparent throughout this book, however, constantly improving technology has made it possible for fewer people to produce what is needed from the goods producing industries. The trend toward more production from fewer people will continue, and the total number of people employed in the goods producing sector will continue to decline. Thus, communities choosing to base their economy on industries with declining employment are placing themselves in a situation in which a vibrant economy is virtually impossible to achieve. It is essential that economic development strategies consist of more than attempting to attract a manufacturing firm to the community.

DOI: 10.7330/9781607329510.c010

A critical factor is that a vibrant economy is a diversified economy. Communities heavily dependent on a single industry or sector are greatly impacted by the unique changes within that business or sector. For example, energy-dependent communities constantly experience a cycle of boom and bust. When energy prices are high, jobs are abundant and wages elevated. When prices decline, however, jobs disappear and wages decline. When the resource is depleted, the jobs are gone. Likewise, amenity and tourism communities tend to create jobs that are low wage and seasonal. Remaining dependent on manufacturing or other goods-producing industries results in a steadily declining workforce.

While amenities, energy, manufacturing, or the resource industries can provide an economic base, a vibrant and resilient community must have significant employment in other sectors that provide stability and offset the variability associated with any particular industry. Rural economic stability and growth are positively associated with economic diversity (Wagner and Deller 1998).

Another thing communities can do to achieve economic vibrancy is to encourage the development of locally owned businesses rather than attracting national chains. When the business is locally owned, profits stay in the community. In contrast, for national chains, revenues are immediately sent away to corporate headquarters. Additionally, local ownership means the person are committed to succeeding in that community, while a national chain will move if the enterprise is not profitable. Similarly, when communities produce more of their food or energy locally, the money that is generated stays in the local community.

Perhaps most important, a vibrant twenty-first-century rural economy must fully utilize modern communication and information technology. It must be based on innovation and knowledge (Moretti 2012). Technological developments that have reduced the cost of distance have opened doors of opportunity for rural communities that simply did not exist in the past. To a greater extent than ever before, individuals and families can live where they wish, instead of being required to live near their place of employment.

Among the many benefits of an economy based on modern information and communication technology is that it simplifies choices for two-career couples. During the latter decades of the twentieth century, Americans were known for moving often. At that time, more than one in five families moved each year.

Finding better employment opportunities was among the more important reasons for moving. Generally, the husband's job was paramount, and the move was made to improve his career opportunities. Upon reaching the new location, the wife would either stay home with the kids or find whatever job she could.

Over the years, the number of dual-career couples in which both partners place a high priority on their careers has increased substantially. This has made moving for career improvement much more difficult. Finding a good job for both partners in the same city is often really hard. This problem is especially pronounced in small rural communities. A move that would benefit one partner may be detrimental to the other. At least partially as a consequence, the proportion of people moving each year is now about one-half of the proportion that were moving previously. From 2015 to 2016, the Census reported that only 11.2 percent of families moved. There is no question that modern information and communication technology can reduce some of this burden faced by two-career couples. In a growing number of cases, either or both members of a couple can find high-quality jobs in a place where they both wish to live by taking advantage of modern information and communication technology.

Another population segment that has trouble moving is single parents. In some cases, moving to another community could enhance employment opportunities, but might entail leaving behind family members who play a critical role in both childcare and emotional support. Again, opportunities for these individuals to find lucrative and meaningful employment where they wish to live are increasingly available as a result of modern information and communication technology.

Finally, there is the significant benefit for people to live where they choose to live. Some people may want to live near family and friends. Some may want to live near amenities that they enjoy. Utilizing modern technology, such choices are much more realistic than in the past.

There are several ways for communities and individuals to achieve a twenty-first-century economy. Some are described below.

## Market Products Globally

Historically, businesses in rural communities were disadvantaged relative to businesses in urban communities because they were distant from large numbers of potential consumers. Transportation costs also put them at a disadvantage. A business operating in a small town either had to sell its products to the much smaller number of local residents or transport them, with the subsequent expenses to urban markets.

In the modern world, by using the computer and the Internet, businesses located anywhere, including rural communities, can market their products to potential consumers anywhere in the world. For example, a company named Triassic in Moab, Utah, uses locally recycled wood and stone to make beautifully handcrafted furniture, jewelry, plates, bowls, and tools. These products are then sold to tourists visiting Moab and also marketed globally on the Internet. In Sheridan, Wyoming, locally produced leather is used to make saddles, shoes, and art products. Again, these products are marketed globally on the Internet.

There are, of course, limitations to the products that can be marketed globally. If a company or farm is producing undifferentiated commodities such as wheat or milk, competition for marketing these products will be global. As a result, the disadvantages inherent in rural areas, such as distance from markets and subsequent transportation costs, will be relevant. In a global marketplace, more undifferentiated commodities than ever before are competing. Because of better information and communication, buyers can be aware of products from all over the world. Thus, local wheat producers now must compete with wheat producers from Ukraine, Australia, or Kansas. The greatest opportunities for rural businesses in a global world will be in marketing unique products such as those being produced in Moab and Sheridan. Perhaps products that are relevant to the community's history or culture may do especially well.

If products such as cheese, honey, or apple juice are produced, it is essential that these products be differentiated and perhaps a brand created and marketed. For example, Cache Valley Cheese and Napa Valley Wine are brands that are well known nationally, and in some cases globally.

## The Virtual Office

For growing numbers of people, it is no longer necessary to be physically present in the office each day. For these individuals, much of the work is done on the computer and using the Internet and can be done as well from home as from the office. More and more of these people have the option of living where they wish and doing their work virtually. A growing number of these people are choosing to live in rural communities. In some cases, individuals may need to travel to the corporate office for an occasional meeting, but they can work from home on a day-to-day basis.

Attracting more of these people presents great economic development opportunities for rural communities. Communities may be able to attract skilled and highly paid individuals to live in their community even though their employer is far away. In general, such people will be a great asset to the community.

Often the virtual office provides advantages for the company as well as for the employee. For example, the company may need a smaller building with fewer offices and a smaller parking lot than they would otherwise. The financial savings are obvious. As a society, we would all benefit from less traffic during rush hour, reduced resource consumption, and less pollution because people are working from home rather than driving to work each day.

Numerous examples exist of people working from their virtual office. Routledge Press, located in London, England, published one of my recent books. The Routledge editor who worked on my book lives in Ohio, as there is no reason that she needs to be in London. In Ohio, she lives near family and friends. She is living near her husband's work, which does require him to be physically present.

Often in my travels I find it necessary to talk on the phone with airline personnel who assist me with complicated or changing flight schedules. When I ask these individuals where they live, answers have included rural Minnesota, rural Tennessee, and rural Arizona. As long as these individuals have a computer and a telephone, persons with these jobs can live virtually anywhere they wish.

I was working in a rural community where one of the community leaders had a job managing the payroll for a university located about 200 miles away. He told me his job was completely computer and Internet based and he would much prefer to live in the small town where he grew up rather than live in the much larger university town. Similarly, I have known software engineers employed by Silicon Valley firms who live in small-town southern Utah and accountants working for a large firm in Denver who live in rural Montana. At a meeting in a small community in the West, I met a woman who teaches online courses for the University of Indiana. Another individual who makes a living by translating Arabic lives in a small town in the West. One of my neighbors is a tax attorney and works for a large Salt Lake City firm. He prefers to live in Cache Valley because it is near family and there is less congestion. In all of these cases, the community benefits from having talented and well-paid individuals living in their community, and they didn't have to attract the industry. Without having the industry, the community doesn't have to worry about subsequent pollution, and so on.

## Lone Eagles and the Creative Class

There have always been people with jobs that Richard Florida (2002) defines as "creative class." These include writers and artists who can live anywhere they wish. Rural areas are high on the list of where many of these people wish to live, as they feel that they can do their job better from a place that is quiet and peaceful. Often high-quality amenities are also among the reasons people chose to live where they do. For example, John Grisham has homes in Oxford, Mississippi, and outside of Charlottesville, Virginia; Stephen King lives in Bangor, Maine; and Stephenie Meyer lives in Cave Creek, Arizona. As was the case with the virtual office people, a rural community may benefit greatly by attracting these types of people.

Most likely opportunities for creative class persons will continue to grow. As the number of people needed in the goods producing industries decline, more people will be free to provide creative and unique services to those who can afford to pay for these services. Many of these opportunities have not even been imagined yet, and the range of potential opportunities is limited only by our creativity.

## The Growing Market for Freelancers

With the advent of modern information and communication technology, many companies no longer find it necessary to hire a person to do some of the tasks that need to be completed. Instead, they can contract with a freelancer to do the work. For example, many small businesses need help with designing and updating their web page. Often, however, the small business doesn't have the budget or workload to hire a full-time web designer.

Instead, they can hire a freelance web designer and then pay him/her by the task.

A number of websites (such as upload.com) have emerged to connect employers with potential freelance workers. Contact between employer and employee is made online, a contract agreed upon, the work completed, and the freelancer paid for the completed job. The employer and employee may never meet face to face. If the employer likes the work, it could go back to the same freelancer the next time it need work done. If the employee likes working for that business, she or he may accept. In some cases, the relationship may evolve into a regular position. The employer may use the piecework with the freelancer as an extended job interview.

The size of the freelance economy is large and becoming even larger. It is estimated that in 2017, over 57 million people worked as freelancers. Based on current trends, it is expected that by 2027 the majority of workers will be freelancers. The range of potential jobs for freelancers is vast, and may include writers, customer service agents, website designers, administrative support, and accountants.

Freelancing provides benefits for both the employer and the employee. The employer can get needed work completed without hiring an employee. The savings could be substantial, as the employer may not need a full-time person and it doesn't have to provide benefits. The freelance employees can choose the jobs they want and avoid those they don't want, they can choose when to work and when not to work, and they can choose where they wish to live. The potential of living where one wishes is especially beneficial for rural areas, since people can live there and work for employees who may be anywhere in the world.

Freelancing also has a number of drawbacks. Significantly, most freelance workers do not have health insurance or retirement as is common for people with regular full-time jobs. In addition, for freelance workers there is inherent instability of not knowing where next month's or next year's paycheck will come from. Freelance workers will have to have enough restraint to withhold funds to pay taxes when they come due. For these reasons, freelancing may work best where one member of a couple has regular full-time employment with benefits while the other complements the family income with freelance work. This arrangement would provide the benefits of allowing the couple to live where they wish.

## Value Added

The most fundamental aspect of economic growth involves taking resources and rearranging them in ways that make them more valuable. Traditionally, rural communities have produced raw materials, such as wheat and trees, that were then exported and the value added was provided in other communities. These other communities then received the major economic gains. Through value-added industries, jobs are created and a much higher proportion of the economic benefits stay in the rural community. Opportunities to benefit from value-added are much greater in the modern world because products can be advertised and marketed globally on the Internet.

## Changes Necessary for a Twenty-First-Century Economy

At one time, workers lacking an advanced education or high-level skills could obtain a job in the goods producing industries. As I was growing up, I was often told that anyone willing to work hard could make a good living. With recent economic structure changes, this is no longer the case. Specifically, there has been a significant decline in the number of jobs available for persons with a high school degree or less. A critical aspect of current economic structure changes is that the importance of education has increased. Technological developments have replaced many of the low-skill jobs in the goods producing industries. At the same time the need for skilled workers in information and data analysis has grown. Since the beginning of the 2007–2009 recession, there has been a significant growth in the number of jobs for persons with a bachelor's degree or higher. In contrast, there are millions fewer jobs for persons with a high school degree or less than at the beginning of the 2007–2009 recession.

Not only has the number of jobs for low-skilled workers declined, but also have pay levels for remaining low-skill jobs. One reason is that jobs for low-skilled workers in the goods producing industries pay more than low-skill jobs in other sectors, especially the service sector. Basically, this is a consequence of low-skill service workers (such as those working in service industries such as a fast food restaurant) earning less than low-skill factory workers, loggers, or miners. Table 10.1 shows that persons with a college degree earn nearly four times more than persons who have not completed high school. At the same time, 26.3 percent of persons with less than a high school education

**TABLE 10.1.** Income and Poverty Levels by Educational Attainment, 2016

|  | Less than High School | High School Graduate | Some College | College Graduate School |
|---|---|---|---|---|
| Median Household Income | $27,868 | $43,331 | $59,048 | $97,072 |
| Percent in Poverty | 26.3 | 12.9 | 9.6 | 4.5 |

*Source:* Semega et al. 2017.

live in poverty, compared to only 4.5 percent of college graduates. The consequence is that the jobs skills required by workers of the future will be different from job skills that previously allowed people to earn a comfortable livelihood. Young people need to be prepared for a world very different from their parent's world, and many older workers need training to learn a new set of skills. This shift is significant because the number of low-skill workers in the goods producing industries has been declining, while the number of low-skill workers in the service industries has been growing, at least temporarily. Another factor is that reduced employment in the goods producing industries has resulted in reduced power of unions, which results in lower incomes.

To summarize, workers wishing to earn a livable income in the new information and service economy will need more education and training than in the past. The importance of a college degree or postgraduate degree is increasing. Every year since 1973, the gap in wages between a person with a college degree and a person without a college degree has been increasing (McCall 2000). As a consequence, young people need to understand that it is essential that they get some type of education and training beyond high school. Additionally, for many older workers it will be necessary to obtain additional education or training to make them competitive in obtaining a job in the new era. Greatly needed are policies to make education and training beyond high school more affordable. This includes education and training both for young people just out of high school and for older workers whose job skills have been made obsolete by changing technology.

## The Role of the Nation, State, and Community

Public entities have a vital role in creating a vibrant twenty-first-century economy at the local level. Some of things that could be done at each level of government are described in the following sections.

*National Government*

A first and critically vital step is assuring that high-speed Internet is available to all Americans, regardless of location. Currently, the quality of Internet varies widely from one place to another (Whitacre et al. 2015) and is generally much worse in rural areas compared to urban areas. I have visited rural areas where the quality of Internet is atrocious. In some small towns, my cell phone is of little more value than to be a paperweight. This weakness is largely a consequence of financial decisions made by the telecom industry. These companies are motivated to provide high-quality Internet to urban areas where the number of potential customers is large. The telecoms are much less motivated to run costly cable to rural areas where there are few customers and thus little return on their investment. There is no way to achieve high-quality Internet to everyone without significant public expenditure. To be effective, these expenditures must come from the federal government. Our country has a precedent with rural electrification that occurred during the 1930s where federal expenditures made possible the provision of electricity to rural Americans. The same commitment is needed now to provide high-quality Internet to all Americans.

The federal government can play a role in the provision of other infrastructure as well. Additionally, funding and programs to make advanced education affordable to persons from all segments of society would be extremely valuable.

*State Government*

The training and skills needed to earn a living in a modern world based on an information and knowledge economy are very different from those needed in previous eras. Specifically, the proportion of the workforce that needs a college education is much greater than in the past. The costs of a college education have increased considerably in recent years, making it very difficult for persons from the working and lower classes to attend and complete college. The costs of an advanced education for individuals have increased because the state has been unwilling to pay the same proportion of these costs that they were willing to pay in the past. Thinking of my own situation, my family was not in position to provide much help with college expenses, but programs were available in that era to provide grants and loans for students such as me. In addition, tuition was much cheaper than it is now, and I always had a part-time job. The consequence was that I was able to earn both undergraduate and graduate degrees. No question, because I have been able to earn higher wages than I would have been able to earn otherwise, I have paid back in taxes the funds that were given to me again and again. In other words, public investment in my education was a profitable decision for policy makers.

Many universities are establishing branch campuses in locations throughout their state. In some cases, the local extension offices are made available so that individuals can watch and participate in a course whose instructor is at the school's main campus. Both approaches have proven to be extremely helpful for persons desiring to advance their education who find it difficult to spend several years at the universities' main campuses. For example, I have interacted with several couples in their thirties. Circumstances vary, but typically one spouse has a good job in the local community while the other spouse is entering or returning to the workforce, or has watched her or his current job skills become obsolete as a result of technological change. Moving the family to a university town to complete college is not feasible. Attending college classes at a branch campus, however, makes attainment of the needed additional education possible.

College may not be for everyone. Even those who do not go to college need training and skills beyond high school. Again, the state can provide affordable training to help people become electricians, plumbers, mechanics, medical assistants, and numerous other occupations. Workforce training centers and community colleges can not only be helpful for young people needing additional training, but also play a vital role in retraining adults who have found their job skills made obsolete by economic restructuring.

### Local Governments

There is also much that city and county governments can do to help their residents obtain the skills necessary to attain high-quality employment in a twenty-first-century economy. For example, classes and workshops that teach skills to help people more effectively use modern information and communication technology are greatly needed. Communities could establish mentoring programs in which people with expertise can help those who would like to gain that expertise. Further, at present, access to high-speed Internet is often lacking in many homes, especially in rural areas. Communities could help by making public spaces available that have high-speed Internet for individuals to work at freelance or similar occupations. For example, computers that are connected to high-speed Internet could be placed at the public library or space made available at the public schools. Communities can also use available resources to encourage the development of a twenty-first-century economy, rather than using scarce resources in an attempt to rebuild an economy that worked in the 1960s.

## Conclusions

The economy has changed dramatically in recent decades, and these trends will continue. Because of technological developments, employment in the goods producing industries will continue to decline. Rather than attempting to rebuild an economy that worked in the past, rural communities must seek to establish a modern twenty-first-century economy. The ideas described in this book are the path to make this possible. If this path is followed, the future of rural communities can be bright.

# References

Abatzoglou, J. T., J.F.C. DiMento; P. Doughman, and S. Nespor. 2014. "A Primer on Global Climate-Change Science." In *Climate Change: What It Means for Us, Our Children, and Out Grandchildren*, edited by J.F C. DiMento and P. Doughman., chap. 2. Boston: MIT Press.

Abbey, Edward. 1968. *Desert Solitaire*. New York: McGraw-Hill.

Albrecht, Don E. 2004. "Amenities, Natural Resources, Economic Restructuring and Socioeconomic Outcomes in Nonmetropolitan America." *Journal of the Community Development Society* 35(2): 36–52.

Albrecht, Don E. 2012. "A Comparison of Metro and Nonmetro Incomes in a Twenty-First Century Economy." *Journal of Rural Social Sciences* 27(1): 1–23.

Albrecht, Don E. 2014a. *Rethinking Rural: Global Community and Economic Development in the Small Town West*. Pullman: Washington State University Press.

Albrecht, Don E., ed. 2014b. *Our Energy Future: Socioeconomic Implications and Policy Options for Rural America*. New York: Routledge.

Albrecht, Don E. 2019. "The Rural Vote and the Election of Donald Trump." *Journal of Rural Social Sciences* 34(1): article 3.

Albrecht, Don E., Carol M. Albrecht, and Stan L. Albrecht. 2000. "Poverty in Nonmetropolitan America: Impacts of Industrial, Employment and Family Structure Variables." *Rural Sociology* 65(1): 36–52.

DOI: 10.7330/9781607329510.c011

Albrecht, Don E., and Steve H. Murdock. 1990. *The Sociology of U.S. Agriculture: An Ecological Perspective*. Ames: Iowa State University Press.

Allen-Diaz, Barbara. 1995. *Rangelands in a Changing Climate: Impacts, Adaptations, and Mitigation*. London: Provided for Intergovernmental Panel on Climate Change Working Group.

Anderson, T. L., L. E. Huggins, and T. M. Power, eds. 2008. *Accounting for Mother Nature*. Stanford, CA: Stanford University Press.

Autor, David, and David Dorn. 2013. "The Growth of Low-Skill Service Jobs and the Polarization of the U.S. Labor Market." *American Economic Review* 103(5): 1553–1597.

Autor, David, Lawrence F. Katz, and Melissa S. Kearney. 2008. "Trends in U.S. Wage Inequality: Revising the Revisionists." *Review of Economics and Statistics* 90(2): 300–323.

Beck, J. L., and D. L. Mitchell. 2000. "Influences of Livestock Grazing on Sage Grouse Habitat." *Wildlife Society Bulletin* 28(4): 993–1002.

Belton, L. R., and D. Jackson-Smith. 2010. "Factors Influencing Success among Collaborative Sage-Grouse Management Groups in the Western United States." *Environmental Conservation* 37(3): 250–260.

Benson, Michael L., Greer Fox, Alfred DeMaris, and Judy Van Wyk. 2003. "Neighborhood Disadvantage, Individual Economic Distress and Violence Against Women in Intimate Relationships." *Journal of Quantitative Criminology* 19(3): 207–235.

Berkman, Lisa F. and Ichiro Kawachi. 2000. *Social Epidemiology*. New York: Oxford University Press.

Beyers, W., and P. Nelson. 2000. "Contemporary Development Forces in the Nonmetropolitan West: New Insights from Rapidly Growing Communities." *Journal of Rural Studies* 16(4): 459–474.

Bluestone, Barry, and Bennett Harrison. 1982. *The Deindustrialization of America*. New York: Basic Books.

Boal, William M. 2009. "The Effect of Unionism on Accidents in U.S. Coal Mining, 1897–1929." *Industrial Relations* 48(1): 97–120.

Booth, Alan, and Paul Amato. 1991. "Divorce and Psychological Stress." *Journal of Health and Social Behavior* 32(December): 396–407.

Boyle, P., and K. Halfacree. 1998. *Migration into Rural Areas*. Chichester, UK: Wiley.

Brick, Howard. 1998. *Age of Contradiction*. Ithaca, NY: Cornell University Press.

Brockerhoff, Eckehard G., H. Jactel, J. A. Parrotta, C. P. Quine, and J. Sayer. 2008. "Plantation Forests and Biodiversity: Oxymoron or Opportunity?" *Biodiversity and Conservation* 17(5): 925–951.

Brown, R. B., S. F. Dorins, and R. S. Krannich. 2005. "The Boom-Bust-Recovery Cycle: Dynamics and Change in Community Satisfaction and Social Integration in Delta, Utah." *Rural Sociology* 70(1): 28–49.

Brulle, R. J., J. Carmichael, and J. C. Jenkins. 2012. "Shifting Public Opinion on Climate Change: An Empirical Assessment of Factors Influencing Concern over Climate Change in the US, 2002–2010." *Climatic Change* 114(2): 169–188.

Byrne, J. M., and R. J. Sampson. 1986. *The Social Ecology of Crime.* New York: Springer-Verlag.

Carmichael, J. T., and R. J. Brulle. 2017. "Elite Cues, Media Coverage, and Public Concern: An Integrated Path Analysis of Public Opinion on Climate Change, 2001–2013." *Environmental Politics* 26(2): 232–252.

Carson, Rachel. 1962. *Silent Spring.* Boston: Houghton Mifflin.

Carter, Bill. 2012. *Boom, Bust, Boom.* New York: Scribner.

Case, Anne, and Angus Deaton. 2015. "Rising Morbidity and Mortality in Midlife among White Non-Hispanic Americans in the 21st Century." *Proceedings of the National Academy of Sciences of the United States of America* 112(49): 15078–15083.

Caudill, Harry M. 1963. *Night Comes to Cumberlands.* New York: Little, Brown and Company.

Cawley, R. McGreggor. 1993. *Federal Land, Western Anger: The Sagebrush Rebellion and Environmental Politics.* Lawrence: University Press of Kansas.

Chetty, Raj, Nathaniel Hendren, Patrick Kline, and Emmanuel Saez. 2014. *Where Is the Land of Opportunity? The Geography of Intergenerational Mobility in the United States.* National Bureau of Economic Research Working Paper No. 19843.

Chevan, A., and R. Stokes. 2000. "Growth in Family Income Inequality, 1970–1990: Industrial Restructuring and Demographic Change." *Demography* 37(3): 365–380.

Christopherson, Susan, and Ned Rightor. 2014. "Confronting an Uncertain Future: How U.S. Communities are Responding to Shale Gas and Oil Development." *Our Energy Future: Socioeconomic Implications and Policy Options for Rural America*, edited by D. E. Albrecht, chap. 3. New York: Routledge.

Clark, Anna. 2018. *The Poisoned City.* New York: Macmillan.

Clary, David. 1986. *Timber and the Forest Service.* Lawrence: University Press of Kansas.

Clifford, Hal. 2002. "Last Dance for the Sage Grouse." *High Country News* 34(2): 8–12.

Cochrane, Willard W. 1979. *The Development of American Agriculture: A Historical Analysis.* Minneapolis: University of Minnesota Press.

Connelly, J. W., Steven T. Knick, Michael A. Schroeder, and San J. Stiver. 2004. "Conservation Assessment of Greater Sage-Grouse and Sagebrush Habitats." Cheyenne, WY: Western Association of Fish and Wildlife Agencies.

Connelly, J. W., M. A. Schroeder, A. R. Sands, and C. E. Braun. 2000. "Guidelines to Manage Sage Grouse Populations and Their Habitats." *Wildlife Society Bulletin* 28(December): 967–985.

Cramer, Katherine. 2016. *The Politics of Resentment: Rural Consciousness in Wisconsin and the Rise of Scott Walker.* Chicago: University of Chicago Press.

Crawford, John A., R. A. Olson, N. E. West, J. C. Mosley, M. A. Schroeder, T. D. Whitson, R. F. Miller, M. A. Gregg, and C. S. Boyd. 2004. "Ecology and

Management of Sage-Grouse and Sage-Grouse Habitat." *Rangeland Ecology and Management* 57(1): 2–19.

Cromartie, John. 2009. *Baby Boom Migration and Its Impact on Rural America*. ERS Economic Research Report No. 79. Washington, DC: USDA, Economic Research Service.

Cromartie, J. B., and J. W. Wardwell. 1999. "Migrants Settling Far and Wide in the Rural West." *Rural Development Perspectives* 14(2): 1–8.

Culhane, Paul J. 2013. *Public Lands Politics: Interest Group Influence on the Forest Service and the Bureau of Land Management*. New York: Routledge.

Cunfer, Geoff. 2005. *On the Great Plains: Agriculture and Environment.*College Station: Texas A&M University Press.

Danziger, S., and P. Gottschalk. 1995. *America Unequal*. Cambridge, MA: Harvard University Press.

Darby, Kaye. 1967. *The Emergence of the Large Lumber Producers and Their Significance to the Lumber Industry*. MS thesis, Portland State University.

Davis, Charles, ed. 2001. *Public Lands and Environmental Politics*. 2nd ed. Boulder, CO: Westview.

Desmond, Matthew. 2016. *Evicted*. New York: Penguin Random House.

Dietrich, William. 1992. *The Final Forest*. New York: Simon and Schuster.

DiMento, J.F P., and P. Doughman, eds. 2014. *Climate Change: What It Means for Us, Our Children, and Our Grandchildren*. Cambridge, MA: MIT Press.

Donahue, Debra L. 1999. *The Western Range Revisited*. Norman: University of Oklahoma Press.

Duffy-Deno, Kevin T. 1998. "The Effect of Federal Wilderness on County Growth in the Intermountain Western United States." *Journal of Regional Science* 38(1): 109–136.

Duncan, Cynthia M. 1999. *Worlds Apart: Why Poverty Persists in Rural America*. New Haven, CT: Yale University Press.

Dunlap, R. E., and A. M. McCright. 2008. "A Widening Gap: Republican and Democratic Views on Climate Change." *Environment* 50(5): 26–35.

Eisenhauer, Brian W., Richard S. Krannich, and Dale J. Blahna. 2000. "Attachments to Special Places on Public Lands: An Analysis of Activities, Reason for Attachments, and Community Connections." *Society and Natural Resources* 13(5): 421–441.

Ellsworth, William L. 2013. "Injection-Induces Earthquakes." *Science* 341 (6142): 1225942.

Emanuel, Kerry. 2012. *What We Know about Climate Change*. 2nd ed. Cambridge, MA: MIT Press.

Farrigan, Tracey. 2015. *Geography of Poverty*. Washington, DC: Economic Research Service, USDA.

Fernandez-Cornejo, Jorge. 2007. "Farmers Balance Off-Farm Work and Technology Adoption." *Amber Waves* 5(1): 23–27.

Fernando, Felix, Anne Junod, Jeffrey Jacquet, Robert Hearne, and Lynette Flage. 2018. "Housing Challenges and Policy Implications of Shale Oil Development in Rural Communities." In *Rural Housing and Economic Development*. Edited by Don E. Albrecht, Scott Loveridge, Stephan Goetz, and Rachel Welborn, chap. 11. London: Routledge.

Ferrell, S. L., and L. Sanders. 2013. "Natural Gas Extraction: Issues and Policy Options." NARDeP Report (nardep.info).

FitzGerald, Frances. 2017. *The Evangelicals: The Struggle to Shape America*. New York: Simon and Schuster.

Fitzgerald, Timothy. 2014. "Property Rights for Hydraulic Fracturing." NARDeP Policy Brief No. 23 (nardep.info).

Florida, Richard. 2002. *The Rise of the Creative Class*. New York: Basic Books.

Fortmann, Louise, and S. K. Fairfax. 1991. "Forest Resource Policy." In *Rural Policies for the 1990s*, edited by C. B. Flora and J. A. Christenson, chap. 22. Boulder, CO: Westview Press.

Frank, Thomas. 2004. *What's the Matter with Kansas?* New York: Henry Holt and Company.

Frentz, Irene, Frank Farmer, James M. Gulden, and Kimberly G. Smith. 2004. "Public Lands and Population Growth." *Society and Natural Resources* 17(1): 57–68.

Freudenburg, W. R., R. Gramling, and D. J. Davidson. 2008. "Scientific Certainty Argumentation Methods (SCAMS)." *Sociological Inquiry* 78(1): 2–38.

Fuguitt, G. V., D. L. Brown, and C. L. Beale. 1989. *Rural and Small Town America*. New York: Russell Sage.

Galbraith, John Kenneth. 1958. *The Affluent Society*. Boston: Houghton Mifflin.

Gaspar, J., and E. Glaeser. 1998. "Information Technology and the Future of Cities." *Journal of Urban Economics* 43(1): 136–156.

Gentner, B. J., and J. A. Tanaka. 2002. "Classifying Federal Public Land Grazing Permittees." *Journal of Range Management* 55(1): 2–11.

Giddens, A. 2009. *The Politics of Climate Change*. Malden, MA: Polity Press.

Gilens, Martin. 1999. *Why American Hate Welfare*. Chicago: University of Chicago Press.

Glaeser, E. 2011. *Triumph of the City: How Our Greatest Invention Makes Us Richer, Smarter, Greener, Healthier and Happier*. New York: Penguin Press.

Gold, Russell. 2014. *The Boom*. New York: Simon and Schuster.

Goldstein, Amy. 2017. *Janesville: An American Story*. New York: Simon and Schuster.

Gosnell, Hannah, and Jesse Abrams. 2011. "Amenity Migration: Diverse Conceptualizations of Drivers, Socioeconomic Dimensions, and Emerging Challenges." *GeoJournal* 76(4): 303–322.

Gosnell, Hannah, and W. R. Travis. 2005. "Ranchland Ownership Dynamics in the Rocky Mountain West." *Rangeland Ecology and Management* 58(2): 191–198.

Grann, David. 2017. *Killers of the Flower Moon: The Osage Murders and the Birth of the FBI*. New York: Doubleday.

Green, Gary P. 2001. "Amenities and Community Economic Development: Strategies for Sustainability." *Journal of Regional Analysis and Policy* 31(1): 61–75.

Hagen, Christian A., John W. Connelly, and Michael A. Schroeder. 2007. "A Meta-Analysis of Greater Sage-Grouse Centrocercus Urophasianus Nesting and Brood-Rearing Habitats." *Wildlife Biology* 13(Sp1): 42–50.

Hamilton, C. 2007. *Scorcher: The Dirty Politics of Climate Change.* Melbourne: Black Inc.

Hansen, A. J., R. Rasker, B. Maxwell, J. J. Rotella, J. D. Johnson, A. D. Parmenter, U. Langer, W. B. Cohen, R. L. Lawrence, and M. Kraska. 2002. "Ecological Causes and Consequences of Demographic Change in the New West." *BioScience* 52(2): 151–162.

Hansen, A. J., R. L. Knight, J. M. Marzluff, S. Powell, K. Brown, P. H. Gude, and K. Jones. 2005. "Effects of Exurban Development on Biodiversity: Patterns, Mechanisms, and Research Needs." *Ecological Applications* 15(6): 1893–1905.

Hardin, Garrett. 1968. "The Tragedy of the Commons." *Science* 162(3859): 1243–1248.

Hassol, S. J. 2004. *Impacts of a Warming Arctic: Arctic Climate Impact Assessment.* New York: Cambridge University Press.

Haveman, R., B. Wolfe, and K. Pence. 2001. "Intergenerational Effects of Nonmarital and Early Childbearing." In *Out of Wedlock*, edited by L. L. Wu and B. Wolfe, chap. 10. New York: Russell Sage Foundation.

Haven, Jennifer R., C. B. Oser, H. K. Knudsen, M. Lofwall, W. W. Stoops, S. L. Walsh, C. J. Leukefeld, and A. H. Kral. 2011. "Individual and Network Factors Associated with Non-Fatal Overdose among Rural Appalachian Drug Users." *Drug and Alcohol Dependence* 115(1): 107–112.

Hays, Samuel P. 2007. *Wars in the Woods.* Pittsburgh: University of Pittsburgh Press.

Hays, Samuel P. 2009. *The American People: The National Forests.* Pittsburgh: University of Pittsburgh Press.

Hedges, Chris. 2010. "Democracy in America Is a Useful Fiction." *truthdig.com. Drilling Beneath the Headlines* (January).

Helfield, James M., and Robert J. Naiman. 2001. "Effects of Salmon-Derived Nitrogen on Riparian Forest Growth and Implications for Stream Productivity." *Ecology* 82(9): 2403–2409.

Henderson, J., and K. McDaniel. 1998. "Do Scenic Amenities Foster Economic Growth in Rural Areas?" *Regional Economic Digest* 1: 11–17.

Hertz, Thomas, Lorin Kusmin, Alexander Marré, and Timothy Parker. 2014. *Rural Employment Trends in Recession and Recovery.* Washington, DC: USDA, Economic Research Service.

Hicks, M. J., and S. Devaraj. 2015. *The Myth and Reality of Manufacturing in America.* Muncie, IN: Center of Business and Economic Research, Ball State University.

Hochschild, Arlie Russell. 2016. *Strangers in Their Own Land.* New York: New Press.

Holloran, Matthew J., and Stanley H. Anderson. 2005. "Spatial Distribution of Greater Sage-Grouse Nests in Relatively Contiguous Sagebrush Habitats." *Condor* 107(4): 742–752.

Holmes, P., and W. Hecox. 2004. "Does Wilderness Impoverish Rural Areas?" *International Journal of Wilderness* 10(3): 34–39.

Houghton, J. T., Y. Ding, D. J. Griggs, M. Noguer, P. J. van der Linden and D. Xiaosu. 2001. *Climate Change 2001: The Scientific Basis.* Contribution of Working Group I to the Third Assessment Report of the intergovernmental Panel on Climate Change (IPCC). Cambridge: Cambridge University Press.

Hulme, M. 2009. *Why We disagree about Climate Change.* New York: Cambridge University Press.

Hunter, Lori M., Jason D. Boardman, and Jarron M. Saint Onge. 2005. "The Association between Natural Amenities, Rural Population Growth and Long-Term Residents' Economic Well-Being." *Rural Sociology* 70(4): 452–69.

Hyde, Charles K. 1998. *Copper for America.* Tucson: University of Arizona Press.

IPCC (Intergovernmental Panel on Climate Change). 2014. *Fifth Assessment Report of the Intergovernmental Panel on Climate Change.* New York: Cambridge University Press.

Jackson-Smith, Douglas, E. Jensen, and B. Jennings. 2006. "Changing Land Use in the Rural Intermountain West." In *Population Change and Rural Society* (Volume 16), edited by W. A. Kandel and D. L. Brown, chap. 12. New York: Springer Science and Business Media.

Jakus, Paul M. 2016. *What Does the Quality of Public Land Imply for Federal Land Transfers.* Western Policy Brief. Logan, Utah: Western Rural Development Center.

Jakus, Paul M., Jan E. Stambro, Michael Hogue, John Downen, Levi Pace, and Therese C. Grijalva. 2017. "Western Public Lands and the Fiscal Implications of a Transfer to States." *Land Economics* 93(August): 371–389.

Johansen, H. E., and G. V. Fuguitt. 1984. *The Changing Rural Village in America: Demographic and Economic Trends since 1950.* Cambridge, MA: Ballinger Publishing Company.

Johnson, Kenneth M., and Daniel T. Lichter. 2019. "Rural Depopulation: Growth and Decline Processes over the Past Century." *Rural Sociology* 84(1): 1–25.

Kelly, E. C., and J. C. Bliss. 2009. "Healthy Forests, Healthy Communities: An Emerging Paradigm for Natural Resource-Dependent Communities?" *Society and Natural Resources* 22(6): 519–537.

Kenny, Kevin. 1998. *Making Sense of the Molly Maguires.* New York: Oxford University Press.

Kingsolver, Barbara. 1989. *Holding the Line: Women in the Great Arizona Mine Strike of 1983.* Ithaca, NY: ILR Press.

Kohrs, El Dean. 1974. "Social Consequences of Boom Growth in Wyoming." Paper presented at the annual meetings of the Rocky Mountain Section of the American Association for the Advancement of Science, Laramie, Wyoming.

Krugman, P. 1991. "Increasing Returns and Economic Geography." *Journal of Political Economy* 99(3): 483–499.

Lachapelle, Paul, and Don Albrecht. 2019. *Addressing Climate Change at the Community Level in the United States.* London: Routledge.

Lahsen, M. 2005. "Technocracy, Democracy, and U.S. Climate Politics." *Science, Technology and Human Values* 30(1): 137–169.

Lahsen, M. 2008. "Experiences of Modernity in the Greenhouse: A Cultural Analysis of the Physicists 'Trio' Supporting the Backlash against Global Warming." *Global Environmental Change* 18(1): 204–219.

Layzer, J. 2007. "Deep Freeze." In *Business and Environmental Policy,* edited by M. E. Kraft and S. Kamieniecki, 93–125. Cambridge, MA: MIT Press.

Leiserowitz, A., E. Maibach, C. Roser-Renouf, G. Feinberg, and S. Rosenthal. 2017. "Climate Change in the American Mind: October, 2015." Report. New Haven, CT: Yale University and George Mason University, Yale Program on Climate Change Communication.

LeMonds, James. 2001. *Deadfall: Generations of Logging in the Pacific Northwest.* Missoula, MT: Mountain Press Publishing.

Libecap, Gary D. 1993. *Contracting for Property Rights.* New York: Cambridge University Press.

Lindberg, T. T., E. S. Bernhardt, R. Brier, A. M. Helton, R. B. Merola, A. Vengosh, and R. T. Di Giulio. 2011. "Cumulative Impacts of Mountaintop Mining on an Appalachian Watershed." *Proceedings of the National Academy of Sciences* 108(52): 20929–20934.

Lindenmayer, David B., and Jerry F. Franklin. 2002. *Conserving Forest Biodiversity: A Comprehensive Multiscaled Approach.* Washington, DC: Island Press.

Lorah, P., and R. Southwick. 2003. "Environmental Protection, Population Change, and Economic Development in the Rural Western United States." *Population and Environment* 24: 255–272.

Low, Sarah. 2017. "Rural Manufacturing Survival and Its Role in the Rural Economy." *Amber Waves* 1490-2017-3200.

Mayer, Jane. 2016. *Dark Money.* New York: Doubleday.

McCall, Leslie. 2000. "Gender and the New Inequality: Explaining the College/Non-College Wage Gap." *American Sociological Review* 65: 234–255.

McCright, A. M. 2007. "Dealing with Climate Change Contrarians." In *Creating a Climate for Change: Communicating Climate Change and Facilitating Social Change,* edited by S. C. Moser and L. Dilling, 200–212. New York: Cambridge University Press.

McCright, A. M., and R. E. Dunlap. 2000. "Challenging Global Warming as a Social Problem: An Analysis of the Conservative Movement's Counter Claims." *Social Problems* 47(4): 400–522.

McCright, A. M., and R. E. Dunlap. 2003. "Defeating Kyoto: The Conservative Movement's Impact on U.S. Climate Change Policy." *Social Problems* 50(3): 348–373.

McCright, A. M., and R. E. Dunlap. 2011a. "The Politicization of Climate Change and Polarization in the American Public's Views of Global Warming, 2001–2010." *Sociological Quarterly* 52(2): 155–194.

McCright, A. M., and R. E. Dunlap. 2011b. "Cool Dudes: The Denial of Climate Change among Conservative White Males in the United States." *Global Environmental Change* 21(4): 1163–1172.

McGranahan, D. A. 1999. *Natural Amenities Drive Rural Population Change.* Agricultural Economic Report No. 781. Washington, DC: Economic Research Service, US Department of Agriculture.

McGranahan, D. A. 2009. "Scenic Landscapes Enhance Rural Growth." *Amber Waves* (June): 9.

McGranahan, D. A., and T. R. Wojan. 2007. "The Creative Class: A Key to Rural Growth." *Amber Waves* (April): 17–21.

Merrill, Karen R. 2002. *Public Lands and Political Meaning.* Berkeley: University of California Press.

Metcalf, Gilbert E. 2009. "Designing a Carbon Tax to Reduce U.S. Greenhouse Gas Emissions." *Review of Environmental Economics and Policy:* 1–22.

Monnat, Shannon. 2018. "Drug Overdose Rates Are Highest in Places with the Most Economic and Family Distress." *Carsey Research National Issue Brief #134.* Carsey School of Public Policy, University of New Hampshire.

Monnat, S. M., and K. K. Rigg. 2016. "Examining Rural/Urban Differences in Prescription Opioid Misuse among US Adolescents." *Journal of Rural Health* 32(2): 204–218.

Moretti, Enrico. 2012. *The New Geography of Jobs.* Boston: Houghton Mifflin Harcourt.

Muratori, Matteo. 2014. "Rural Energy Use and the Challenges for Energy Conservation and Efficiency." In *Our Energy Future: Socioeconomic Implications and Policy Options for Rural America*, edited by D. E. Albrecht, chap. 8. New York: Routledge.

Naugle, David E., ed. 2011. *Energy Development and Wildlife Conservation in Western North America.* Washington, DC: Island Press.

Nelson, Robert H. 1995. "The Federal Land Management Agencies." In *A New Century for Natural Resources Management*, edited by R. L. Knight and S. F. Bates, chap. 2. Washington, DC: Island Press.

Neiwert, David. 2017. *Alt-America.* London: Verso.

Newell, Frederick H. 1896. "Irrigation on the Great Plains." *Yearbook of the United States Department of Agriculture.* Washington, DC: US Department of Agriculture.

Nie, Martin. 2008. *The Governance of Western Public Lands.* Lawrence: University of Kansas Press.

Nord, M., and J. B. Cromartie. 1997. "Migration: The Increasing Importance of Rural Natural Amenities." *Choices* 316(2016–7450): 31–32.

Oliver, LeAnn M. 2013. "The Energy Future of Rural America." *Rural Connections* 7(2): 3–6.

Oreskes, N., and E. M. Conway. 2008. "Challenging Knowledge: How Climate Science Became a Victim of the Cold War." In *Agnotology: The Making and Unmaking of Ignorance*, edited by R. N. Proctor and L. Schiebinger, 55–89. Stanford, CA: Stanford University Press.

Oreskes, N., and E. M. Conway. 2010. *Merchants of Doubt*. New York: Bloomsbury Press.

Otterstrom, S. M., and J. M. Shumway. 2003. "Deserts and Oases: The Continuing Concentration of Population in the American Mountain West." *Journal of Rural Studies* 19(4): 445–462.

Paarlberg, Don. 1980. *Farm and Food Policy: Issues of the 1980s*. Lincoln: University of Nebraska Press.

Palmer, M. A., E. S. Bernhardt, W. H. Schlesinger, K. N. Eshleman, E. Foufoula-Georgiou, M. S. Hendrix, A. D. Lemly, G. E. Likens, O. L. Loucks, M. E. Power, and P. S. White. 2010. "Mountaintop Mining Consequences." *Science* 327(5962): 148–149.

Pellant, Mike. 1996. *Cheatgrass: The Invader that Won the West*. Boise: Bureau of Land Management, Idaho State Office.

Powell, James Lawrence. 2011. *The Inquisition of Climate Science*. New York: Columbia University Press.

Prugh, Laura R., C. J. Stoner, C. W. Epps, W. T. Bean, W. J. Ripple, A. S. Laliberte, and J. S. Brashares. 2009. "The Rise of the Mesopredator." *Bioscience* 59(9): 779–791.

Quadagno, Jill. 1994. *The Color of Welfare: How Racism Undermined the War on Poverty*. New York: Oxford University Press.

Rahm, D. 2010. *Climate Change Policy in the United States*. Jefferson, NC: McFarland.

Rasker, Ray. 2017. *The Changing Role of Manufacturing in the U.S. and Insights for the Rural West*. Bozeman, Montana: Headwater Economics.

Rasker, Ray, and Andrew Hansen. 2000. "Natural Amenities and Population Growth in the Greater Yellowstone Region." *Human Ecology Review* 7(2): 30–40.

Resnick, Michael D., P. S. Bearman, R. W. Blum, K. E. Bauman, K. M. Harris, J. Jones, J. Tabor, T. Beuhring, R. E. Sieving, M. Shew, and M. Ireland. 1997. "Protecting Adolescents from Harm: Findings from the National Longitudinal Study on Adolescent Health." *Journal of the American Medical Association* 278(10): 823–832.

Righter, Robert W. 1989. "National Monuments to National Parks: The Use of the Antiquities Act of 1906." *The Western Historical Quarterly* 1989: 201–301.

Robinson, Glen O. 1975. *The Forest Service: A Study in Public Land Management*. Washington, DC: Resources for the Future.

Rosenblum, Jonathan D. 1995. *Copper Crucible*. Ithaca, NY: ILR Press.

Rosenzweig, Cynthia, D. Karoly, M. Vicarelli, P. Neofotis, Q. Wu, G. Casassa, and A. Menzel. 2008. "Attributing Physical and Biological Impacts to Anthropogenic Climate Change." *Nature* 453(7193): 353–357.

Rudzitis, Gundars. 1999. "Amenities Increasingly Draw People to the Rural West." *Rural Development Perspectives* 14(2221-2019-2682): 9–13.

Rudzitis, Gundars, and H. E. Johansen. 1991. "How Important Is Wilderness? Results from a United States Survey." *Environmental Management* 15(2): 227–233.

Saint Onge, J. M., L. M. Hunter, and J. D. Boardman. 2007. "Population Growth in High Amenity Rural Areas." *Social Science Quarterly* 88(2): 366–381.

Sassen, S. 1990. "Economic Restructuring and the American City." *Annual Review of Sociology* 16(1): 465–490.

Schroeder, M. A., J. R. Young, and C. E. Braun. 1999. "Sage Grouse (*Centrocercus urophasianus*)." In *The Birds of North America*, No. 425, edited by A. Poole and F. Gill, 28. Philadelphia: Birds of North America.

Semega, Jessica L., Kayla R. Fontenot, and Melissa Kollar. 2017. *Income and Poverty in the United States: 2016*. P60–259. Washington, DC: U. S. Census Bureau.

Sergio, Fabrizio, Ian Newton, and Luigi Marchesi. 2005. "Conservation: Top Predators and Biodiversity." *Nature* 436(7048): 192–192.

Sergio, Fabrizio, T. Caro, D. Brown, B. Clucas, J. Hunter, J. Ketchum, K. McHugh, and F. Hiraldo. 2008. "Top Predators as Conservation Tools: Ecological Rationale, Assumptions, and Efficacy." *Annual Review of Ecology, Evolution, and Systematics* 39: 1–19.

Serreze, M. C., J. E. Walsh, F. S. Chapin, T. Osterkamp, M. Dyurgerov, V. Romanovsky, W. C. Oechel, J. Zhang, and R. G. Barry. 2000. "Observational Evidence of Recent Change in the Northern High-Latitude Environment." *Climatic Change* 46(1–2): 159–-207.

Shearman, D. J., and J. W. Smith. 2007. *The Climate Challenge and the Failure of Democracy*. London: Praeger.

Sherman, Jennifer. 2005. *Men without Sawmills: Masculinity, Rural Poverty, and Family Stability*. Rural Poverty Research Center Working Paper No. 05–03. Corvallis, OR: RUPRI.

Sherman, Jennifer. 2006. "Coping with Rural Poverty: Economic Survival and Moral Capital in Rural America." *Social Forces* 85(2): 891–913.

Sherman, Jennifer. 2009. *Those Who Work, Those Who Don't: Poverty, Morality, and Family in Rural America*. Minneapolis: University of Minnesota Press.

Shumway, J. M., and J. A. Davis. 1996. "Nonmetropolitan Population Change in the Mountain West: 1970–1999." *Rural Sociology* 61(3): 513–529.

Shumway, J. M., and S. M. Otterstrom. 2001. "Spatial Patterns of Migration and Income Change in the Mountain West: The Dominance of Service-Based, Amenity-Rich Counties." *Professional Geographer* 53(4): 492–502.

Smith, M. D., and R. S. Krannich. 1998. "Tourism Dependence and Resident Attitudes." *Annals of Tourism Research* 25(4): 783–802.

Smith, M. D., and R. S. Krannich. 2000. "'Culture Clash' Revisited: Newcomers and Longer-Term Residents' Attitudes toward Land Use, Development, and

Environmental Issues in Rural Communities in the Rocky Mountain West." *Rural Sociology* 65(3): 396–421.

Smith, M. D., R. S. Krannich, and L. M. Hunter. 2001. "Growth, Decline, Stability and Disruption: A Longitudinal Analysis of Social Well-Being in Four Western Rural Communities." *Rural Sociology* 66(3): 425–456.

Snyder, Stephen Edward. 2016. "Urban and Rural Divergence in Mortality Trends: A Comment on Case and Deaton." *Proceedings of the National Academy of Sciences of the United States of America* 113(7): E814.

Speth, J. G. 2004. *Red Sky at Morning.* New Haven, CT: Yale University Press.

Squillace, Mark. 2002. "The Monumental Legacy of the Antiquities Act of 1906." *Georgia Law Review* 37: 473.

Steinbeck, John. 1939. *The Grapes of Wrath.* New York: Viking Press.

Stern, Nicholas. 2007. *The Economics of Climate Change.* New York: Cambridge University Press.

Stiglitz, Joseph E. 2012. *The Price of Inequality.* New York: W.W. Norton.

Stiller, David. 2000. *Wounding the West.* Lincoln: University of Nebraska Press.

Stiver, S. J. 2006. *Greater Sage-Grouse Comprehensive Conservation Strategy.* Cheyenne, WY: Western Association of Fish and Wildlife Agencies.

Stoellinger, Temple. 2014. "Implications of a Greater Sage-Grouse Listing on Western Energy Development." NARDeP Policy Brief No. 33 (nardep.info).

Storper, M., and A. Venables. 2004. "Buzz: Face-to-Face Contact and the Urban Economy." *Journal of Economic Geography* 4(4): 351–370.

Tanaka, J. A., N. R. Rimbey, and L. A. Torell. 2014. "Ranching Economics and Sage-Grouse in the West: Policy Recommendations for Rural Development." NARDeP Policy Brief No. 19 (nardep.info).

Torell, L. A., J. A. Tanaka, N. Rimbey, T. Darden, L. Van Tassell, and A. Harp. 2002. *Ranch-Level Impacts of Changing Grazing Policies on BLM Lands to Protect the Greater Sage-Grouse: Evidence from Idaho, Nevada and Oregon.* PACWLP Policy Paper SG-01–02. Caldwell: Policy Analysis Center for Western Public Lands, University of Idaho.

Travis, William R. 2007. *New Geographies of the American West.* Washington, DC: Island Press.

Tyner, Wallace E., and Farzad Teheripour. 2014. "Unconventional Shale Oil and Gas Production and Greenhouse Gas Reduction." *NARDeP*: Policy Brief 21.

Uslaner, Eric M. 1998. "Social Capital, Television, and the 'Mean World': Trust, Optimism and Civic Participation." *Political Psychology* 19(3): 441–467.

Vance, J. D. 2016. *Hillbilly Elegy.* New York: HarperCollins.

Van der Ploeg, F., and A. J. Venables. 2012. "Natural Resource Wealth: The Challenge of Managing a Windfall." *Annual Review of Economics* 4(September): 315–337.

Venables, A. 2003. "Spatial Disparities in Developing Countries: Cities, Regions and International Trade." Working Paper: London School of Economics.

Vias, A. C., and J. I. Carruthers. 2005. "Regional Development and Land Use Change in the Rocky Mountain West." *Growth and Change* 36(2): 244–272.

Wagner, J., and S. Deller. 1998. "Measuring the Effects of Economic Diversity on Growth and Stability." *Land Economics* 74(4): 541–556.

Washington, H., and J. Cook. 2011. *Climate Change Denial*. Washington, DC: Earthscan.

Webb, Walter Prescott. 1931. *The Great Plains*. Boston: Ginn and Company.

Weinstein, Amanda, and Mark Partridge. 2014. "Economic Implications of Unconventional Fossil Fuel Production." In *Our Energy Future: Socioeconomic Implications and Policy Options for Rural America*, edited by D. E. Albrecht, chap. 2. New York: Routledge.

Weiser, Scott. 2018. "How the Gold King Mine Disaster Happened." *Complete Colorado* (June 22).

Wetts, Rachel, and Rob Willer. 2018. "Privilege on the Precipice: Perceived Racial Status Threats Lead White Americans to Oppose Welfare Programs." *Social Forces* 97(2): 793–822.

Whitacre, B., S. Strover, and R. Gallardo. 2015. "How Much Does Broadband Infrastructure Matter? Decomposing the Metro-Nonmetro Adoption Gap with the Help of the National Broadband Map." *Government Information Quarterly* 32(3): 261–269.

Wilkinson, Charles F. 1992. *Crossing the Next Meridian*. Washington, DC: Island Press.

Wilson, W. J. 1987. *The Truly Disadvantaged*. Chicago: University of Chicago Press.

Wilson, W. J. 1996. *When Work Disappears*. New York: Knopf.

Winkler, R., D. R. Field, A. E. Luloff, R. S. Krannich, and T. Williams. 2007. "Social Landscapes of the Intermountain West: A Comparison of 'Old West' and 'New West' Communities." *Rural Sociology* 72(3): 478–501.

Wirth, Louis. 1938. "Urbanism as a Way of Life." *American Journal of Sociology* 44(1): 1–24.

Wunthnow, Robert. 2018. *The Left Behind*. Princeton, NJ: Princeton University Press.

Yergin, Daniel. 2011. *The Quest*. New York: Penguin Press.

Zuckerman, Gregory. 2013. *The Frackers*. New York: Penguin.

# Index

**P**

Pacific Coast, 84, 94
Pacific Northwest, 86, 88, 90, 96, 123
Panguitch, Utah, 155, 156
Paris Agreement, 129, 130
Park City, Utah, 116, 118
Park Service lands, 145
Park Service's Organic Act, 87
Partridge, Mark, 80
Payment in lieu of taxes (PILT), 93
Peabody Energy, 54
Pennsylvania, 3, 29, 48, 50, 54, 68
Permafrost, 127
Permian Basin, West Texas, 72
Pesticides, 32, 124
Petroleum, 47, 48, 51–52, 70, 76
Pikes Peak, 101
PILT (Payment in lieu of taxes), 93
Pinkerton Agency, 17, 18, 50
Pipelines, 68
Pitkin County, Colorado, 115–116, 118
Pittsburgh, Pennsylvania, 18, 25
Plains, 36–37, 38, 39, 42, 43. *See also* Great Plains, The
Plains Indians, 37
"Pockets" of poverty, 18
Polar bears, 130
Policies: to assist rural America, 12–13; beneficial, 132; education and training, 172; environmental, 123, 124–126, 130; federal, 14; harmful effects from, 54, 124, 130, 131, 147, 149, 163; homestead laws, 144; impacts of sage grouse, 139, 140; public land, 146; to strengthen unions, 111; to support resource development, 82, 117
Political polarization, 128
Political power, 12
Pollution: avoiding, 10; coal, 54, 65; contaminated water, 99–100; control laws, 124; costs of energy use, 54; noise, 75; sources, 125
Population: change, 150, 156–157; and climate change, 132; and economic growth, 148–149; single parents, 166; working in tourism, 158
Population, size: advantages, 8; energy consumption, 70; exploded, 75–76, 103, 106; increases and declines in, 80, 94; in urban areas, 9
Population of Baca County, Colorado, 1930–2010, 45

Population of Clallam County, Washington, 1900–2017, 95
Population of Daniels County, Montana, 1930–2010, 41, 41
Population of Garfield County, Utah, 1890–2017, 156
Population of Greenlee County, Arizona, 1920–2017, 109
Population of Pitkin County, Colorado, 1890–2017, 116
Population of Silver Bow County, Montana, 1890–2017, 104
Population of Teton County, Wyoming, 1930–2017, 114
Population trends: in Aspen, 115–116; in Campbell County, Wyoming, 1920–2015, 60; in Carbon county, 62, 62; in Daniels County, 40–41, 43–44; in Flint, 23; in Grand County, 118–119; in Greenlee County, 108; in Kenai Peninsula, 120–121; in Martin County, Kentucky, 57, 57, 58; in McKenzie County, North Dakota, 1910–2017, 81; in Millard County, Utah 1920–2015, 64; in Richland County, Wisconsin, 27; in Teton County, 113–115; in Williams County, North Dakota, 1910–2017, 81; in Youngstown, Ohio, 1880–2017, 21
Population trends in Flint, Michigan, 1880–2017, 24, 27
Population trends in Youngstown, Ohio, 1880–2017, 22
Portland International Airport, 152
Poverty: in Appalachia, 59, 63; coal dependence and, 56; Johnson's War on, 58; living in, 172
Poverty rates, 8, 18, 22, 23
Powder River Basin, 53, 60, 61
Power plants, 52, 55, 60, 63–64, 118
Prairie, 36, 37, 38, 39, 42, 80, 101
Precipitation, 37, 38, 94, 127, 150. *See also* Rainfall
Predators, 36, 135, 136, 137
Presidential proclamations, 153
Price, Utah, 61
Privately owned lands, 87–88, 136, 138
Privatization, opposition to, 147–148
Privilege to own land, 30–31
Production: agricultural, 31; coal, 51–54, 58, 61, 62, 63, 70, 76; copper, 11, 106; crop, 99, 114, 132; crude oil, 68–69, 80, 82; demand for miners, 103; domestic energy, 72, 75; and economic